sweet food

sweet food

MURDOCH
BOOKS

Contents

Baked

Strawberry roulade

2 eggs
1 egg white
125 g (½ cup) caster sugar
90 g (¾ cup) self-raising flour
1 tablespoon caster sugar, extra
250 g (1 cup) smooth ricotta cheese
1 teaspoon vanilla essence
40 g (⅓ cup) icing sugar
250 g (1⅔ cups) strawberries, hulled
   and chopped

Preheat the oven to 200°C (400°F/ Gas 6). Lightly grease a 26 x 30 cm swiss roll tin and line with baking paper, leaving the paper hanging over the two long sides.

Using electric beaters, beat the eggs, egg white and sugar in a large bowl on high speed for 5 minutes, or until light and foamy. Sift the flour into the bowl and fold in quickly and lightly.

Pour the mixture into the prepared tin and smooth the surface. Bake for 8–10 minutes, or until the sponge springs back to the light touch. Lay a sheet of baking paper on a clean tea towel and sprinkle lightly with the extra caster sugar.

Turn the sponge out onto the sugared paper, remove the lining paper and, starting from a short end, roll up the sponge with the paper, using the tea towel as a guide. Cool for 30 minutes.

Mix the ricotta, vanilla and icing sugar together with a wooden spoon. Unroll the sponge and spread with the ricotta mixture, leaving a 2 cm border at the far end. Scatter over the strawberries, then carefully re-roll the sponge. Trim the ends, and cut into slices to serve.

Serves 8

Apricot and macaroon slice

100 g unsalted butter, softened
90 g (⅓ cup) caster sugar
1 egg
185 g (1½ cups) plain flour
½ teaspoon baking powder

Filling
250 g (1⅓ cups) dried apricots,
  roughly chopped
1 tablespoon Grand Marnier
2 tablespoons caster sugar

Topping
100 g unsalted butter
90 g (⅓ cup) caster sugar
1 teaspoon vanilla essence
2 eggs
270 g (3 cups) desiccated coconut
40 g (⅓ cup) plain flour
½ teaspoon baking powder

Preheat the oven to 180°C (350°F/ Gas 4). Lightly grease a 20 x 30 cm baking tin and line with baking paper. Cream the butter and sugar until light and fluffy. Add the egg and beat well. Sift the flour and baking powder and fold into the butter mixture with a metal spoon. Press firmly into the tin and bake for 20–25 minutes, or until golden brown. Cool.

To make the filling, combine the apricots, Grand Marnier, sugar and 125 ml (½ cup) boiling water in a bowl. Set aside for 30 minutes, then purée in a food processor. Spread evenly over the cooled base.

To make the topping, cream the butter, sugar and vanilla until light and fluffy. Gradually add the eggs, beating well after each addition. Fold in the coconut, flour and baking powder with a large metal spoon. Spoon onto the apricot leaving it lumpy and loose — do not press down. Bake for 20–25 minutes, or until lightly golden.

Makes 16 pieces

Orange and almond cake

2 large navel oranges
6 eggs, separated
1 tablespoon orange blossom water
  or orange liqueur
250 g (1 cup) caster sugar
300 g (3 cups) ground almonds
1 teaspoon baking powder
3 navel oranges, peeled, pith and
  sinew removed, thinly sliced,
  to garnish

Orange syrup
500 ml (2 cups) fresh orange juice,
  strained
185 g (³/₄ cup) caster sugar
60 ml (¹/₄ cup) Sauternes

Grease and lightly flour a 23 cm springform cake tin, tipping out any excess flour. Put the whole oranges into a saucepan full of water. Boil for 2 hours, topping up with water as needed. Remove the oranges, quarter them and process in a food processor until smooth. Cool thoroughly. Preheat the oven to 180°C (350°F/Gas 4).

Place the egg yolks, orange blossom water and caster sugar in a large bowl and beat until smooth, then stir in the orange purée and mix well. Whisk the egg whites in a clean, dry bowl until firm peaks form. Add the ground almonds and baking powder to the orange mixture, stir well, then fold in the egg whites. Pour into the cake tin and bake for 1 hour, or until firm — cover with foil if it overbrowns. Cool in the tin, then transfer to a serving plate.

To make the syrup, put the orange juice, sugar and Sauternes in a saucepan over medium heat and stir until the sugar is dissolved. Reduce the heat and simmer for 20 minutes, or until reduced by half and slightly syrupy, skimming off any scum.

Cut the cake into wedges, garnish with orange slices and drizzle with the syrup. Delicious served with cream.

Serves 6–8

Spiced treacle gingerbreads

140 g unsalted butter, cubed and
   softened
115 g (1/2 cup) dark brown sugar
90 g (1/4 cup) treacle, preferably black
1 egg
250 g (2 cups) plain flour
30 g (1/4 cup) self-raising flour
3 teaspoons ground ginger
2 teaspoons ground cinnamon
3/4 teaspoon ground cloves
3/4 teaspoon ground nutmeg
1 teaspoon bicarbonate of soda

Tinted icing
1 egg white
1/2 teaspoon lemon juice
125 g (1 cup) icing sugar, sifted
assorted food colourings

Lightly grease two baking trays. Beat the butter and sugar until light and creamy, then beat in the treacle and egg. Fold in the combined sifted flours, spices and bicarbonate of soda. Turn out onto a lightly floured surface and knead until smooth. Cover with plastic wrap and chill for 10 minutes.

Divide the dough in half and roll out between two sheets of lightly floured baking paper to a 4 mm thickness. Lay the dough on the trays and chill for 15 minutes until just firm. Preheat the oven to 180°C (350°F/Gas 4).

Cut out the dough using a 7 cm heart-shaped cutter. Using a 1 cm plain cutter, cut a hole at the top of each heart. (You can thread these with ribbon to hang up the biscuits.) Lay on the trays and bake for 10 minutes. Leave for 5 minutes, then cool on a wire rack.

To make the icing, whisk the egg white until foamy. Add the lemon juice and sugar and stir until glossy. Tint the icing any colour you want, then spoon into paper piping bags, seal the end and snip off the tip. Decorate the biscuits with the icing.

Makes about 36

Flourless chocolate cake

500 g good-quality dark chocolate,
 chopped
6 eggs
2 tablespoons Frangelico or brandy
165 g (1½ cups) ground hazelnuts
250 ml (1 cup) whipping cream
icing sugar, to dust
thick (double) cream, to serve

Preheat the oven to 150°C (300°F/ Gas 2). Grease a deep 20 cm round cake tin and line the base with baking paper. Place the chocolate in a heatproof bowl. Half fill a saucepan with water, boil, then remove from the heat and sit the bowl over the pan — don't let the bowl touch the water. Stir occasionally until the chocolate melts.

Put the eggs in a large heatproof bowl and add the Frangelico. Put the bowl over a pan of barely simmering water — don't let it touch the water. Beat the mixture with electric beaters on high speed for 7 minutes, or until light and foamy. Remove from the heat.

Using a metal spoon, quickly and lightly fold the chocolate and ground nuts into the egg mixture until just combined. Fold in the whipped cream and pour into the cake tin. Put the cake tin in a shallow roasting tin. Pour hot water into the roasting tin to come halfway up the side of the cake tin. Bake for 1 hour, or until just set. Remove the cake tin from the oven and cool to room temperature. Cover with plastic wrap and refrigerate overnight.

Invert the cake onto a plate, remove the paper and cut into slices. Dust with icing sugar and serve with cream.

Serves 10

Sticky toffee slice

250 g (1⅓ cups) pitted dates,
   roughly chopped
1 teaspoon bicarbonate of soda
215 g unsalted butter
185 g (1½ cups) self-raising flour
1 teaspoon vanilla essence
1 teaspoon baking powder
3 eggs
90 ml (⅓ cup) milk
2 tablespoons soft brown sugar
90 g (¾ cup) icing sugar
90 g (¾ cup) chopped walnuts

Preheat the oven to 180°C (350°F/ Gas 4). Lightly grease a 20 x 30 cm baking tin and line with baking paper, hanging over the two long sides.

Place the dates in a saucepan with 200 ml water, bring to the boil, then reduce the heat and simmer gently for 10 minutes — make sure the water doesn't evaporate completely. Add the bicarbonate of soda and leave to cool.

Place 185 g of the butter, the flour, vanilla essence, baking powder, eggs and 75 ml of the milk in a food processor and mix in short bursts for 1 minute, or until well blended. Add the dates and pulse to blend. Do not overprocess.

Place the mixture in the tin and bake for 20 minutes, or until a skewer inserted in the centre comes out clean. Set aside to cool.

Place the remaining butter and milk and the brown sugar in a pan and heat gently to dissolve the sugar. Add the icing sugar and mix well. Spread over the cooled slice and sprinkle with the walnuts.

Makes 18 pieces

Angel food cake with chocolate sauce

125 g (1 cup) plain flour
250 g (1 cup) caster sugar
10 egg whites, at room temperature
1 teaspoon cream of tartar
1/2 teaspoon vanilla essence

Chocolate sauce
250 g dark chocolate, chopped
185 ml (3/4 cup) cream
50 g unsalted butter, chopped

Preheat the oven to 180°C (350°F/ Gas 4). Have an ungreased angel cake tin ready. Sift the flour and 125 g (1/2 cup) of the sugar four times into a large bowl. Set aside. Beat the egg whites, cream of tartar and 1/4 teaspoon salt in a clean, large bowl with electric beaters until soft peaks form. Gradually add the remaining sugar and beat until thick and glossy.

Add the vanilla essence. Sift half the flour and sugar mixture over the meringue and gently fold into the mixture with a metal spoon. Repeat with the remaining flour and sugar. Spoon into the cake tin and bake for 45 minutes, or until a skewer comes out clean when inserted into the centre of the cake. Gently loosen around the side of the cake with a spatula, then turn the cake out onto a wire rack to cool completely.

To make the sauce, put the chocolate, cream and butter in a saucepan. Stir over low heat until the chocolate has melted and the mixture is smooth. Drizzle over the cake and serve.

Serves 8

Note: Ensure the tin is very clean and not greased or the cake will not rise and will slip down the side of the tin.

Vanilla slice

500 g ready-made puff pastry
250 g (1 cup) caster sugar
90 g (³/₄ cup) cornflour
60 g (½ cup) custard powder
1 litre (4 cups) cream
60 g unsalted butter, cubed
2 teaspoons vanilla essence
3 egg yolks

Icing
185 g (1½ cups) icing sugar
60 g (¼ cup) passionfruit pulp
15 g unsalted butter, melted

Preheat the oven to 210°C (415°F/ Gas 6–7). Lightly grease two baking trays with oil. Line the base and sides of a shallow 23 cm square cake tin with foil, leaving the foil hanging over two opposite sides.

Divide the pastry in half, roll each piece to a 25 cm square 3 mm thick and put on a baking tray. Prick all over with a fork and bake for 8 minutes, or until golden. Trim each pastry sheet to a 23 cm square. Put one sheet top-side-down in the cake tin.

Combine the sugar, cornflour and custard powder in a saucepan. Add the cream, stirring constantly over medium heat for 2 minutes, or until it boils and thickens. Add the butter and vanilla and stir until smooth. Remove from the heat and whisk in the egg yolks until combined. Spread the custard over the pastry in the tin, then cover with the other pastry sheet, top-side-down. Cool completely.

To make the icing, combine the icing sugar, passionfruit pulp and butter in a bowl, and stir until smooth.

Lift the slice out of the tin using the foil as handles. Ice the top and leave to set before cutting with a serrated knife.

Makes 9 pieces

Sponge sandwich with jam and cream

4 eggs
1 teaspoon vanilla essence
125 g (½ cup) caster sugar
60 g (½ cup) self-raising flour
60 g (½ cup) cornflour
2 tablespoons raspberry jam
300 ml (1¼ cups) whipping cream
icing sugar, to dust
coloured cachous, to decorate

Preheat the oven to 180°C (350°F/ Gas 4). Grease two shallow 20 cm sponge tins and line each base with baking paper. Beat the eggs, vanilla and sugar with electric beaters for 5 minutes, or until pale and creamy — the beaters should leave a trail in the mixture.

Sift the flours together on a sheet of baking paper. Gently tip the flour into the egg and sugar mixture and fold quickly and lightly using a large metal spoon — do not overmix or it will lose volume. Divide the mixture evenly between the tins. Bake for 20 minutes, or until a skewer comes out clean when inserted into the centre of each cake. Leave in the tins for 5 minutes, then turn out onto a wire rack to cool completely.

Spread one cake with the raspberry jam and whipped cream, then place the other cake on top. Dust with icing sugar to serve, and if desired, decorate with coloured cachous.

Serves 8

Fig and raspberry cake

185 g unsalted butter
185 g (3/4 cup) caster sugar
1 egg
1 egg yolk
335 g (2 2/3 cups) plain flour
1 teaspoon baking powder
4 figs, quartered
grated zest of 1 orange
200 g (1 2/3 cups) raspberries
2 tablespoons sugar

Preheat the oven to 180°C (350°F/ Gas 4). Cream the butter and sugar in a bowl until light and pale. Add the eggs and beat again. Sift the flour over the bowl and fold in with the baking powder and a pinch of salt. Chill for 15 minutes until firm enough to roll out.

Lightly grease a 23 cm springform tin. Divide the dough in two and roll out one piece large enough to fit the base of the tin. Cover with the figs, orange zest and raspberries. Roll out the remaining dough and fit it over the filling. Lightly brush the dough with water and sprinkle with sugar.

Bake for 30 minutes, or until the top and bottom of the cake are cooked. Poke a skewer into the cake to see if it is ready — there should be no wet cake mixture clinging to the skewer. Serve with cream or mascarpone.

Serves 6

Note: If fresh figs are not available, you can use the same amount of dried figs but you need to rehydrate them first. Simmer them in orange juice for 5 minutes until they are plumped up and soft.

Chocolate caramel slice

200 g plain chocolate biscuits,
  crushed
100 g unsalted butter, melted
2 tablespoons desiccated coconut
125 g unsalted butter, extra
400 ml tin sweetened condensed milk
90 g (1/3 cup) caster sugar
3 tablespoons maple syrup
250 g dark chocolate
2 teaspoons oil

Grease a 30 x 20 cm shallow baking tin and line with baking paper, leaving it hanging over the two long sides.

Combine the biscuits, melted butter and coconut in a bowl, then press into the tin and smooth the surface.

Combine the butter, condensed milk, sugar and maple syrup in a small saucepan. Stir over low heat for 15 minutes, or until the sugar has dissolved and the mixture is smooth, thick and lightly coloured. Remove from the heat and cool slightly. Pour over the biscuit base and smooth the surface. Refrigerate for 30 minutes, or until firm.

Chop the chocolate into small even-sized pieces and place in a heatproof bowl. Bring a saucepan of water to the boil and remove from the heat. Sit the bowl over the saucepan, making sure the bowl doesn't touch the water. Allow to stand, stirring occasionally, until the chocolate has melted. Add the oil and stir until smooth. Spread over the caramel and leave until partially set before marking into 24 triangles. Refrigerate until firm. Cut into triangles before serving.

Makes 24 triangles

Yoghurt cake with syrup

185 g unsalted butter, softened
250 g (1 cup) caster sugar
5 eggs, separated
250 g (1 cup) plain Greek-style
  yoghurt
2 teaspoons grated lemon zest
1/2 teaspoon vanilla essence
280 g (2 1/4 cups) plain flour, sifted
2 teaspoons baking powder
1/2 teaspoon bicarbonate of soda
whipped cream, to serve

Syrup
250 g (1 cup) caster sugar
1 cinnamon stick
4 cm strip lemon zest
1 tablespoon lemon juice

Preheat the oven to 180°C (350°F/ Gas 4) and lightly grease a 20 x 10 cm loaf tin.

Place the butter and sugar in a bowl and beat until light and creamy. Add the egg yolks gradually, beating well after each addition. Stir in the yoghurt, lemon zest and vanilla. Fold in the flour, baking powder and bicarbonate of soda with a metal spoon.

Whisk the egg whites in a clean, dry bowl until stiff, and fold into the mixture. Spoon into the prepared tin and bake for 50 minutes, or until a skewer comes out clean when inserted into the centre of the cake. Cool in the tin for 10 minutes, then turn out onto a wire rack to cool.

Meanwhile, to make the syrup, place the sugar and cinnamon stick in a small saucepan with 185 ml (3/4 cup) cold water. Stir over medium heat until the sugar is dissolved. Bring to the boil, add the lemon zest and juice, then reduce the heat and simmer for 5–6 minutes. Strain.

Pour the syrup over the cake and wait for most of it to be absorbed before serving. Cut into slices and serve warm with whipped cream.

Serves 8–10

Raspberry and coconut slice

280 g (2¼ cups) plain flour
3 tablespoons ground almonds
500 g (2 cups) caster sugar
250 g unsalted butter, chilled
½ teaspoon ground nutmeg
½ teaspoon baking powder
4 eggs
1 teaspoon vanilla essence
1 tablespoon lemon juice
300 g (2½ cups) fresh or thawed
   frozen raspberries
90 g (1 cup) desiccated coconut
icing sugar, to dust

Preheat the oven to 180°C (350°F/ Gas 4). Lightly grease a 20 x 30 cm shallow tin and line with baking paper, hanging over the two long sides.

Sift 220 g (1¾ cups) of the flour into a bowl. Add the ground almonds and 125 g (½ cup) of the caster sugar and stir to combine. Rub the butter into the flour with your fingertips until it resembles fine breadcrumbs. Press the mixture into the tin and bake for 20–25 minutes, or until golden. Reduce the oven to 150°C (300°F/Gas 2).

Sift the nutmeg, baking powder and the remaining flour onto a piece of baking paper. Beat the eggs, vanilla and remaining sugar with electric beaters for 4 minutes, or until light and fluffy. Fold in the flour with a large metal spoon. Stir in the lemon juice, raspberries and coconut and pour over the base.

Bake for 1 hour, or until golden and firm. Chill in the tin, then cut into pieces. Dust with icing sugar.

Makes 30 pieces

Macadamia and white chocolate cookies

180 g (1⅓ cups) macadamia nuts,
  lightly toasted (see page 390)
1 egg
140 g (¾ cup) soft brown sugar
2 tablespoons sugar
1 teaspoon vanilla essence
125 ml (½ cup) oil
60 g (½ cup) plain flour
30 g (¼ cup) self-raising flour
¼ teaspoon ground cinnamon
30 g (½ cup) shredded coconut
130 g (¾ cup) white chocolate bits
  (chocolate chips)

Roughly chop the toasted macadamia nuts and set them aside.

Using electric beaters, beat the egg and sugars in a bowl until light and fluffy. Add the vanilla and oil. Using a wooden spoon, stir in the sifted flours, cinnamon, coconut, macadamia nuts and chocolate, and mix well. Refrigerate for 30 minutes. Preheat the oven to 180°C (350°F/Gas 4). Grease and line two baking trays.

Form rounded tablespoons of the mixture into balls and place on the baking trays, pressing the mixture together with your fingertips if it is crumbly. Bake for 12–15 minutes, or until golden. Cool slightly on the trays, then transfer to a wire rack.

Makes about 25

Variation: Dark chocolate bits can be used instead of white chocolate.

Date chocolate torte

100 g (³/₄ cup) slivered almonds
120 g dark chocolate, coarsely
  chopped
120 g (²/₃ cup) dried dates, pitted
3 egg whites
125 g (½ cup) caster sugar
125 ml (½ cup) whipping cream
2 teaspoons caster sugar, extra
30 g dark chocolate, grated, extra

Preheat the oven to 180°C (350°F/ Gas 4). Grease a 22 cm springform tin and line with foil. Chop the almonds and chocolate in a food processor until fine. Finely chop the dates with a sharp knife.

Beat the egg whites with electric beaters until soft peaks form. Slowly add the sugar and continue beating until it dissolves. Fold in the almond and chocolate mixture, then the dates. Spoon the mixture into the prepared tin and level the surface. Bake for 30–35 minutes, or until set and it starts to come away from the side. Cool in the tin before carefully turning out onto a serving plate.

To serve, whip the cream and extra sugar until soft peaks form. Spread the cream evenly over the top with a spatula. Sprinkle with the grated chocolate to decorate.

Serves 6

Note: This is great served for a special afternoon tea or as a dessert. Storage: This torte keeps well, without cream, for 5–6 days wrapped in foil. With cream, this is best eaten on the day of baking.

Pecan brownies

125 g dark chocolate
90 g unsalted butter, softened
250 g (1 cup) caster sugar
1 teaspoon vanilla essence
2 eggs
80 g (2/3 cup) plain flour
30 g (1/4 cup) cocoa powder
1/2 teaspoon baking powder
125 g (1 cup) roughly chopped
   pecan nuts

Preheat the oven to 180°C (350°F/ Gas 4). Grease a 17 cm square tin and line the base with baking paper, hanging over two opposite sides.

Chop the chocolate into small even-sized pieces and place in a heatproof bowl. Bring a saucepan of water to the boil and remove from the heat. Sit the bowl over the pan — ensure the bowl doesn't touch the water. Stand, stirring occasionally, until melted. Cool slightly.

Beat the butter, sugar and vanilla with electric beaters until thick and creamy. Beat in the eggs one at a time, beating well after each addition. Stir in the chocolate.

Fold in the sifted combined flour, cocoa and baking powder with a metal spoon, then fold in the pecans. Spoon into the tin and smooth the surface. Bake for 30–35 minutes, or until firm and it comes away from the sides of the tin. Cool in the tin, remove and cut into squares.

Makes 16 pieces

Zucchini and walnut cake

245 g (2½ cups) walnuts
500 g zucchini (courgettes)
250 ml (1 cup) canola oil
330 g (1½ cups) raw sugar
3 eggs
310 g (2½ cups) self-raising flour,
   sifted
1½ teaspoons ground cinnamon
1 teaspoon ground nutmeg

Preheat the oven to 170°C (325°F/ Gas 3). Grease a 22 x 12 cm loaf tin and line the base and two long sides with a sheet of baking paper.

Roughly chop 185 g (1¾ cups) of the walnuts. Grate the zucchini, then put the zucchini in a large bowl with the oil, sugar, eggs and chopped walnuts and mix well. Stir in the flour, cinnamon and nutmeg.

Spoon the mixture into the tin and arrange the remaining walnuts on top. Bake for 1 hour 10 minutes, or until a skewer comes out clean when inserted into the centre of the cake. Leave in the tin for 20 minutes before turning out onto a wire rack to cool. Cut into slices and serve.

Serves 6–8

Storage: Wrap in foil when cooled. The cake will keep for 4–5 days.

Coconut and pineapple slice

20 g (⅓ cup) shredded coconut
90 g (¾ cup) self-raising flour
50 g (½ cup) plain flour
140 g (¾ cup) soft brown sugar
2 tablespoons sunflower seeds
2 tablespoons sesame seeds
70 g (½ cup) chopped macadamia
  nuts
60 g (⅓ cup) chopped dates
1 tablespoon chopped glacé ginger
45 g (½ cup) desiccated coconut
230 g tin crushed pineapple, drained
100 g unsalted butter, melted
2 eggs, lightly beaten

Icing
250 g (2 cups) icing sugar
30 g unsalted butter, melted
1½ tablespoons lemon juice

Preheat the oven to 170°C (325°F/ Gas 3). Spread the coconut evenly on a baking tray and toast for 5–8 minutes, or until lightly golden. Grease a 20 x 30 cm shallow baking tin and line with enough baking paper to overlap on the longer sides — this will make the slice easier to remove once baked.

Sift the self-raising and plain flours into a large bowl. Add the brown sugar, seeds, macadamia nuts, dates, ginger and desiccated coconut. Stir in the pineapple, melted butter and beaten egg, and mix well.

Spoon the mixture into the prepared tin. Bake for 25–30 minutes, or until golden brown. Cool in the tin, remove and cover with the icing.

To make the icing, combine the icing sugar, melted butter and lemon juice in a small bowl. Stir in 1–2 teaspoons of boiling water to reach a smooth consistency. Spread evenly over the slice. Sprinkle the top with the toasted shredded coconut and when set, slice and serve.

Makes 24 pieces

Note: Use other nuts or seeds, such as pumpkin seeds or almonds, if desired.

Hawaiian macadamia cake

375 g (3 cups) self-raising flour
1 teaspoon ground cinnamon
375 g (1½ cups) caster sugar
90 g (1 cup) desiccated coconut
5 eggs, lightly beaten
440 g tin crushed pineapple in syrup
375 ml (1½ cups) vegetable oil
100 g (⅔ cup) macadamia nuts,
  chopped

Lemon cream cheese icing
60 g (¼ cup) cream cheese, softened
30 g unsalted butter, softened
1 tablespoon lemon juice
185 g (1½ cups) icing sugar, sifted

Preheat the oven to 180°C (350°F/ Gas 4). Grease a 23 cm round deep cake tin. Line the base and side with two sheets of baking paper, cutting it to sit 2–3 cm above the side of the tin.

Sift the flour and cinnamon into a large bowl, add the sugar and coconut and stir to combine. Add the eggs, pineapple and oil and mix well. Stir in the macadamia nuts.

Spoon the mixture into the prepared tin and level the surface. Bake for 1 hour 15 minutes, or until a skewer comes out clean when inserted into the centre of the cake — cover with foil if it browns too much. Leave in the tin for 30 minutes before turning out onto a wire rack.

To make the lemon cream cheese icing, beat the cream cheese and butter in a small bowl. Add the lemon juice and icing sugar and beat until smooth. Spread over the cooled cake.

Serves 10–12

Madeira cake

180 g unsalted butter, softened
185 g (³/₄ cup) caster sugar
3 eggs, beaten
165 g (1 ⅓ cups) self-raising flour,
   sifted
2 teaspoons finely grated lemon zest
1 teaspoon lemon juice
2 teaspoons caster sugar, extra,
   to sprinkle
icing sugar, to dust
lemon zest, extra, to garnish

Preheat the oven to 160°C (315°F/ Gas 2–3). Grease and flour a deep 18 cm round cake tin, shaking out any excess.

Beat the butter and sugar with electric beaters until pale and creamy. Add the eggs gradually, beating well after each addition. Fold in the flour, lemon zest and juice until combined. When smooth, spoon into the prepared tin and level the surface. Sprinkle the extra caster sugar over the top.

Bake for 1 hour, or until a skewer comes out clean when inserted into the centre of the cake. Allow to cool for 15 minutes in the tin before turning out onto a wire rack. To serve, dust with icing sugar and garnish with lemon zest.

Serves 6

Storage: This will keep for 4 days wrapped in foil.

Ginger cheesecake slice

200 g ginger-flavoured biscuits, finely
    crushed
60 g unsalted butter, melted
1/2 teaspoon ground cinnamon
500 g (2 cups) cream cheese
125 ml (1/2 cup) golden syrup
2 tablespoons caster sugar
2 eggs, lightly beaten
55 g (1/4 cup) finely chopped
    crystallized ginger
125 ml (1/2 cup) whipping cream,
    lightly whipped
125 ml (1/2 cup) whipping cream, extra
2 teaspoons caster sugar, extra
55 g (1/4 cup) crystallized ginger, extra,
    thinly sliced

Preheat the oven to 170°C (325°F/
Gas 3). Lightly grease a 20 x 30 cm
baking tin and line with baking paper,
leaving the paper hanging over the
two long sides.

Combine the biscuits, butter and
cinnamon and press into the base of
the tin. Refrigerate for 30 minutes, or
until firm.

Beat the cream cheese, golden syrup
and sugar with electric beaters until
light and fluffy. Add the eggs, one at a
time, beating well after each addition.
Fold in the ginger and lightly whipped
cream. Spread over the base and
bake for 25 minutes, or until just set.
Turn off the oven and cool with the
door slightly ajar.

Remove from the tin and trim the
edges. Beat the extra cream and
extra sugar until soft peaks form and
spread over the cheesecake. Using a
hot dry knife, cut into three strips
lengthways and then cut each strip
into eight pieces. Decorate with the
extra ginger.

Makes 24 pieces

Individual white chocolate chip cakes

125 g unsalted butter, softened
185 g (³/₄ cup) caster sugar
2 eggs, lightly beaten
1 teaspoon vanilla essence
250 g (2 cups) self-raising flour, sifted
125 ml (¹/₂ cup) buttermilk
280 g (1²/₃ cups) white chocolate bits
  (chocolate chips)
white chocolate, shaved, to decorate

White chocolate cream cheese icing
100 g white chocolate
60 ml (¹/₄ cup) cream
200 g (³/₄ cup) cream cheese,
  softened
40 g (¹/₃ cup) icing sugar

Preheat the oven to 170°C (325°F/ Gas 3). Lightly grease twelve 125 ml (¹/₂ cup) muffin tins.

Beat the butter and sugar in a large bowl with electric beaters until pale and creamy. Gradually add the egg, beating well after each addition. Add the vanilla essence and beat until combined. Fold in the flour alternately with the buttermilk, then fold in the chocolate bits.

Fill each muffin hole three-quarters full with the mixture and bake for 20 minutes, or until a skewer comes out clean when inserted into the centre of each cake. Leave in the tins for 5 minutes before turning out onto a wire rack to cool — loosen around the edges if the cakes stick to the tins.

To make the icing, melt the chocolate and cream in a small saucepan over low heat until smooth. Cool slightly, then add to the cream cheese and icing sugar and beat until smooth. Spread the icing over the cakes and garnish with white chocolate shavings

Makes 12

Date caramel shortcake

125 g unsalted butter, softened
125 g (1/2 cup) caster sugar
1 teaspoon vanilla essence
1 egg
250 g (2 cups) plain flour
1 teaspoon baking powder
175 g (1 cup) roughly chopped
  seedless dates
1 tablespoon soft brown sugar
2 teaspoons cocoa powder
10 g unsalted butter, extra
icing sugar, to sprinkle

Preheat the oven to 180°C (350°F/ Gas 4). Lightly grease an 18 x 27 cm shallow baking tin. Line with baking paper, leaving it hanging over the two long sides.

Beat the butter, sugar and vanilla with electric beaters until light and fluffy. Beat in the egg, then transfer to a bowl. Fold in the combined sifted flour and baking powder in batches with a metal spoon.

Press half the dough into the tin. Form the other half into a ball, cover and refrigerate for 30 minutes.

Place the dates, brown sugar, cocoa, extra butter and 250 ml (1 cup) water in a small saucepan. Bring to the boil, stirring, then reduce the heat and simmer, stirring, for 12–15 minutes, or until the dates are soft and the water has been absorbed. Spread onto a plate and refrigerate to cool quickly.

Spread the filling over the pastry base with a metal spatula, then grate the remaining dough over the top. Bake for 35 minutes, or until light brown and crisp. Cool in the tin for 15 minutes, then lift onto a wire rack. Sprinkle with icing sugar and cut into squares.

Makes 12 pieces

Crackle cookies

125 g unsalted butter, cubed and
  softened
370 g (2 cups) soft brown sugar
1 teaspoon vanilla essence
2 eggs
60 g dark chocolate, melted
80 ml (1/3 cup) milk
340 g (2 3/4 cups) plain flour
2 tablespoons cocoa powder
2 teaspoons baking powder
1/4 teaspoon ground allspice
85 g (2/3 cup) chopped pecan nuts
icing sugar, to coat

Lightly grease two baking trays. Beat
the butter, sugar and vanilla until light
and creamy. Beat in the eggs, one at
a time. Stir the chocolate and milk
into the butter mixture.

Sift the flour, cocoa, baking powder,
allspice and a pinch of salt into the
butter mixture and mix well. Stir the
pecans through. Refrigerate for at
least 3 hours, or overnight.

Preheat the oven to 180°C (350°F/
Gas 4). Roll tablespoons of the
mixture into balls and roll each in the
icing sugar to coat.

Place well apart on the trays. Bake
for 20–25 minutes, or until lightly
browned. Leave for 3–4 minutes, then
cool on a wire rack.

Makes about 60

Chocolate banana cake

3 ripe bananas, mashed (about 1 cup)
185 g ($^3/_4$ cup) caster sugar
185 g (1 $^1/_2$ cups) self-raising flour
2 eggs, lightly beaten
3 tablespoons light olive oil
60 ml ($^1/_4$ cup) milk
100 g dark chocolate, grated
90 g ($^3/_4$ cup) walnuts, chopped

Preheat the oven to 180°C (350°F/ Gas 4). Grease a 20 x 10 cm loaf tin and line the base with baking paper.

Mix the mashed banana and sugar in a large bowl until just combined. Add the sifted flour, eggs, oil and milk. Stir the mixture gently for 30 seconds with a wooden spoon. Fold in the chocolate and walnuts.

Pour the mixture into the tin and bake for 55 minutes, or until a skewer comes out clean when inserted into the centre of the cake. Leave to cool in the tin for 5 minutes before turning onto a wire rack. If desired, serve warm with cream.

Serves 6–8

Note: In warm weather, chocolate can be grated more easily if it is left to harden in the freezer for a few minutes before grating.

Fig and cinnamon slice

125 g unsalted butter, softened
55 g (¼ cup) soft brown sugar,
   firmly packed
1 teaspoon ground cinnamon
185 g (1½ cups) plain flour
375 g (2⅓ cups) dried figs
1 cinnamon stick
125 g (½ cup) caster sugar

Preheat the oven to 180°C (350°F/
Gas 4). Lightly grease an 18 x 27 cm
baking tin and line with baking paper,
hanging over the two long sides.

Beat the butter, brown sugar and
cinnamon until light and fluffy, then
fold in the flour with a large metal
spoon. Press the mixture evenly
into the tin and bake for 25 minutes.
Cool slightly.

Place the dried figs, cinnamon stick,
sugar and 375 ml (1½ cups) boiling
water in a saucepan, mix together
and bring to the boil. Reduce the heat
and simmer for 20 minutes, or until
the figs have softened and the water
has reduced by a third. Remove the
cinnamon stick and place the mixture
in a food processor. Process in short
bursts until smooth.

Pour onto the cooked base and bake
for 10 minutes, or until set. Cool in the
tin, then lift out and cut into squares.

Makes 15 squares

Lemon stars

125 g unsalted butter, cubed and
  softened
125 g (½ cup) caster sugar
2 egg yolks
2 teaspoons finely grated lemon zest
155 g (1¼ cups) plain flour
110 g (¾ cup) coarse cornmeal
icing sugar, to dust

Preheat the oven to 160°C (315°F/
Gas 2–3). Line a baking tray with
baking paper. Beat the butter and
sugar until creamy. Mix in the egg
yolks, lemon zest, flour and cornmeal
until they form a ball of soft dough.
Roll out on a lightly floured surface to
1 cm thick.

Cut out stars from the dough using a
3 cm star-shaped cutter. Place on the
tray and bake for 15–20 minutes, or
until lightly golden. Cool on a wire
rack and dust with the icing sugar.

Makes about 22

Pineapple pecan cake

80 g unsalted butter, softened
250 g (1 cup) sugar
2 eggs, lightly beaten
185 g (1 1/2 cups) plain flour
1 3/4 teaspoons baking powder
40 g (1/3 cup) finely chopped pecan
  nuts, toasted
180 g (3/4 cup) finely chopped glacé
  pineapple
170 ml (2/3 cup) milk

Preheat the oven to 180°C (350°F/ Gas 4). Grease a 23 cm round cake tin and line the base with baking paper. Beat the butter and sugar with electric beaters until combined. Add the egg and beat until pale and creamy.

Sift together the flour, baking powder and 1/4 teaspoon salt. Add to the butter mixture with the pecans, pineapple and milk, then beat on low for 1 minute, or until almost smooth.

Spoon the mixture evenly into the prepared tin and smooth the surface. Bake for 1 hour, or until a skewer comes out clean when inserted into the centre of the cake. Leave in the tin for 10 minutes before turning onto a wire rack to cool. If desired, dust with icing sugar just before serving.

Serves 8–10

Note: Glacé pineapple is available from health food stores.

Shredded pastries with almonds

250 g unsalted butter, melted
125 g (1 cup) ground pistachios
230 g (2 cups) ground almonds
625 g (2½ cups) caster sugar
1 teaspoon ground cinnamon
¼ teaspoon ground cloves
1 tablespoon brandy
1 egg white, lightly beaten
500 g kataifi pastry (Greek shredded
    pastry), left at room temperature for
    2 hours (in its packaging)
1 teaspoon lemon juice
5 cm strip lemon zest
4 cloves
1 cinnamon stick
1 tablespoon honey

Preheat the oven to 170°C (325°F/ Gas 3). Brush a 20 x 30 cm baking tray with some melted butter. Put the nuts in a bowl with 125 g (½ cup) of the caster sugar, cinnamon, cloves and brandy. Add the beaten egg white and stir to make a paste. Divide the mixture into eight portions — form each into a 'sausage' about 18 cm long.

Take a small handful of the pastry strands and spread them out fairly compactly with the strands running lengthways towards you. The pastry should measure 25 x 18 cm. Brush with melted butter. Put one of the nut sausages along the end of the pastry nearest to you and roll up into a neat sausage shape. Repeat with the other pastry portions. Place the rolls close together in the baking tray and brush with melted butter. Bake for 50 minutes, or until golden brown.

Place the remaining sugar in a small saucepan with 500 ml (2 cups) water and stir over low heat until dissolved. Add the lemon juice, zest, cloves and cinnamon and boil for 10 minutes. Stir in the honey, then set aside until cold. When the pastries come out of the oven, pour the cold syrup over the top. Leave to cool completely before cutting each roll into 5 pieces.

Makes 40 pieces

Pecan and orange loaf cake

185 g (¾ cup) caster sugar
140 g unsalted butter, softened
2 eggs, lightly beaten
100 g (¾ cup) ground pecan nuts
1 tablespoon grated orange zest
185 g (1½ cups) self-raising flour
125 ml (½ cup) milk
125 g (1 cup) icing sugar

Preheat the oven to 180°C (350°F/ Gas 4). Grease a 22 x 12 cm loaf tin and line the base and the two long sides of the tin with baking paper.

Beat the sugar and 125 g of the butter with electric beaters until pale and creamy. Gradually add the eggs, beating well after each addition. Add the pecans and 3 teaspoons of the orange zest, then gently fold in the sifted flour with a metal spoon alternately with the milk. Spoon the mixture into the prepared tin and smooth the surface.

Bake for 50–60 minutes, or until a skewer comes out clean when inserted into the centre of the cake. Leave in the tin for 10 minutes before turning onto a wire rack to cool.

To make the icing, place the icing sugar, the remaining orange zest and 1–2 tablespoons hot water in a bowl and mix until smooth and combined. Spread the icing over the cooled cake with a flat-bladed knife.

Serves 8–10

Poppy seed slice

135 g (1 cup) plain flour
75 g unsalted butter, chilled and
  chopped
60 g (¼ cup) caster sugar
1 egg yolk
40 g (¼ cup) poppy seeds
2 tablespoons milk, warmed
125 g unsalted butter, extra
90 g (⅓ cup) caster sugar, extra
1 teaspoon finely grated lemon zest
1 egg
90 g (¾ cup) plain flour, extra, sifted
125 g (1 cup) icing sugar
½ teaspoon finely grated lemon zest,
  extra
1 tablespoon lemon juice

Preheat the oven to 180°C (350°F/
Gas 4). Grease an 11 x 35 cm loose-
based flan tin. Sift the flour into a bowl
and rub in the butter with your fingers
until it resembles breadcrumbs. Stir in
the sugar. Make a well in the centre
and add 2–3 teaspoons water and the
egg yolk. Mix with a flat-bladed knife,
using a cutting action until it comes
together in beads. Press into a ball
and flatten slightly. Cover in plastic
wrap and chill for 15 minutes.

Roll out the dough to fit the base and
sides of the tin. Trim the edges. Blind
bake the pastry for 10 minutes (see
page 392), then remove the paper
and beads and bake for 5 minutes, or
until the pastry is dry. Cool.

Soak the poppy seeds in the milk
for 10 minutes. Beat the extra butter
and sugar and the zest until light and
fluffy. Beat in the egg and stir in the
poppy seed mixture and extra flour.
Spread over the pastry and bake for
25 minutes, or until light brown and
cooked through. Cool in the tin until
just warm.

Combine the icing sugar, extra zest
and enough juice to form a paste.
Spread over the slice and cool.

Makes 14 pieces

Beer cake

125 g (1 cup) plain flour
½ teaspoon ground cinnamon
750 g (3 cups) caster sugar
275 g unsalted butter, chopped
3 eggs
500 g (4 cups) self-raising flour
120 g (1 cup) sultanas
500 ml (2 cups) beer
thick (double) cream, to serve

Preheat the oven to 180°C (350°F/ Gas 4). Grease a deep 25 cm round cake tin and line the base with baking paper. To make the topping, mix together the plain flour, cinnamon and 250 g (1 cup) of the sugar. Place in a food processor with 125 g of the butter and combine.

Place the remaining butter in a large bowl with the remaining sugar and beat with electric beaters until pale and creamy. Gradually add the eggs, beating well after each addition — the mixture may look curdled but once you add the flour, it will bring it back together. Fold in the sifted flour, sultanas and beer.

Pour the mixture into the prepared tin and clump the topping together in your hands to form small balls, then sprinkle over the cake. Bake for 1 hour 50 minutes, or until a skewer comes out clean when inserted into the centre. Leave to cool in the tin before inverting onto a wire rack. If desired, serve with cream.

Serves 12

Butterfly cupcakes

120 g unsalted butter, softened
180 g (³/₄ cup) caster sugar
185 g (1¹/₂ cups) self-raising flour
125 ml (¹/₂ cup) milk
2 eggs
125 ml (¹/₂ cup) thick (double) cream
1¹/₂ tablespoons strawberry jam
icing sugar, to dust

Preheat the oven to 180°C (350°F/ Gas 4). Line a flat-bottomed 12-hole cupcake tray with paper patty cases.

Beat the butter, sugar, flour, milk and eggs with electric beaters on low speed. Increase the speed and beat until smooth and pale. Divide evenly among the cases and bake for 30 minutes, or until cooked and golden. Transfer to a wire rack to cool.

Cut shallow rounds from the centre of each cake using the point of a sharp knife, then cut in half. Spoon 2 teaspoons cream into each cavity, top with 1 teaspoon jam and position two halves of the cake tops in the jam to resemble butterfly wings. Dust with icing sugar.

Makes 12

Note: If using foil patty cases instead of the standard paper cases as suggested, the size and number of butterfly cakes may vary.

Strawberry and mascarpone slice

175 g unsalted butter, softened
70 g (⅓ cup) caster sugar
1 egg yolk
250 g (2 cups) plain flour, sifted
300 g (1⅓ cups) mascarpone
60 g (½ cup) icing sugar, sifted
1 tablespoon lemon juice
300 g (2 cups) strawberries, cut
  into quarters
50 g dark chocolate

Preheat the oven to 180°C (350°F/ Gas 4). Lightly grease a 20 x 30 cm shallow baking tin and line with baking paper, leaving it hanging over the two long sides.

Beat the butter and sugar with electric beaters until light and fluffy. Add the egg yolk and beat well. Fold in the sifted flour until well combined. Press firmly into the prepared baking tin and prick all over with a fork. Bake for 25 minutes, or until light brown. Cool completely.

Beat the mascarpone, icing sugar and juice with a wooden spoon until smooth. Stir in the strawberries. Spoon over the base and refrigerate for 3 hours, or until firm.

Chop the chocolate into small even-sized pieces and place in a heatproof bowl. Bring a saucepan of water to the boil, then remove from the heat. Sit the bowl over the pan — ensure the bowl doesn't touch the water. Stand, stirring occasionally, until the chocolate has melted. Drizzle over the slice, then cut into pieces.

Makes 24 pieces

Chocolate ginger and fig cake

125 g unsalted butter, softened
230 g (1 cup) firmly packed soft
  brown sugar
2 eggs, lightly beaten
185 g (1 1/2 cups) self-raising flour
40 g (1/3 cup) cocoa powder
185 ml (3/4 cup) milk
125 g (2/3 cup) dried figs, chopped
75 g (1/3 cup) glacé ginger, chopped

Preheat the oven to 180°C (350°F/ Gas 4). Grease a 22 x 12 cm loaf tin and line the base with baking paper. Beat the butter and sugar with electric beaters until pale and creamy.

Gradually add the egg, beating well after each addition. Stir in the sifted flour and cocoa alternately with the milk to make a smooth batter. Fold in the figs and half the ginger.

Spoon the mixture into the prepared tin and smooth the surface. Scatter the remaining ginger over the top. Bake for 1 hour, or until a skewer comes out clean when inserted into the centre of the cake. Leave the cake to cool in the tin for 5 minutes before inverting onto a wire rack.

Serves 8

Madeleines

3 eggs
100 g (½ cup) caster sugar
150 g (1¼ cups) plain flour
100 g unsalted butter, melted
grated zest of 1 lemon and 1 orange

Preheat the oven to 200°C (400°F/ Gas 6). Brush a tray of madeleine moulds with melted butter and coat with flour, then tap the tray to remove the excess flour.

Whisk the eggs and sugar until the mixture is thick and pale and the whisk leaves a trail when lifted. Gently fold in the flour, then the melted butter and grated lemon and orange zest. Spoon into the moulds, leaving a little room for rising. Bake for 12 minutes (small madeleines will only need 7 minutes), or until very lightly golden and springy to the touch. Remove from the tray and cool on a wire rack.

Makes 14 (or 30 small ones)

Chocolate mud cake

125 g (1 cup) plain flour
125 g (1 cup) self-raising flour
60 g (½ cup) dark cocoa powder
½ teaspoon bicarbonate of soda
625 g (2¾ cups) sugar
450 g dark chocolate, chopped
450 g unsalted butter
125 ml (½ cup) buttermilk
2 tablespoons oil
2 tablespoons instant espresso coffee
  granules or powder
4 eggs

Preheat the oven to 160°C (315°F/ Gas 2–3). Brush a deep 23 cm square cake tin with melted butter or oil. Line the base and sides with baking paper, extending at least 2 cm above the rim.

Sift the flours, cocoa and bicarbonate of soda into a large bowl. Stir in the sugar and make a well in the centre. Put 250 g of the chocolate and 250 g of the butter in a saucepan. Add 185 ml (¾ cup) of water and stir over low heat until melted. Gradually stir the chocolate mixture into the dry ingredients using a large metal spoon.

Whisk together the buttermilk, oil, coffee and eggs in a large jug and add to the mixture, stirring until smooth. Pour into the tin and bake for 1 hour 40 minutes, or until a skewer comes out clean when inserted in the centre. Cool in the tin, then turn out.

Combine the remaining chocolate and butter in a small pan and stir over low heat until smooth. Cool to room temperature, stirring often, until thick enough to spread. Turn the cake upside down so that the uneven top becomes the base, and spread the icing over the entire cake. Allow the icing to set slightly before serving.

Serves 12

Lemon meringue muffins

215 g (1¾ cups) self-raising flour
185 g (¾ cup) caster sugar
1 egg
1 egg yolk
170 ml (⅔ cup) milk
½ teaspoon vanilla essence
90 g unsalted butter, melted and
  cooled
200 g (⅔ cup) ready-made lemon
  curd
2 egg whites
1 teaspoon caster sugar, extra

Preheat the oven to 200°C (400°F/ Gas 6). Grease 12 regular muffin holes. Sift the flour into a large bowl and stir in 60 g (¼ cup) of the caster sugar. Make a well in the centre. Put a pinch of salt, the egg and egg yolk in a bowl and beat together. Stir in the milk, vanilla and butter. Pour the egg mixture into the well. Fold until just combined — the batter will be lumpy.

Divide the muffin mixture among the holes. Bake for 15 minutes — the muffins will only rise a little. (Leave the oven on.) Cool the muffins in the tin for 10 minutes, then loosen with a knife but leave in the tin. Hollow out the centre of each muffin with a melon baller. Fill a piping bag with the lemon curd and fill the centre of each muffin.

Whisk the egg whites in a clean, dry bowl until firm peaks form. Add a quarter of the remaining sugar at a time, beating well after each addition until firm peaks form. Put a heaped tablespoon of meringue on top of each muffin and form peaks with the back of a spoon. Sprinkle over a little caster sugar and bake for 5 minutes, or until the meringue is golden and crisp. Cool in the tin for 10 minutes, then carefully transfer to a wire rack. Serve warm or at room temperature.

Makes 12 regular muffins

Chocolate truffle macaroon slice

3 egg whites
185 g (³/₄ cup) caster sugar
180 g (2 cups) desiccated coconut
250 g dark chocolate
300 ml (1¼ cups) whipping cream
1 tablespoon cocoa powder

Preheat the oven to 180°C (350°F/ Gas 4). Lightly grease a 20 x 30 cm shallow baking tin and line with baking paper, leaving it hanging over the two long sides.

Beat the egg whites in a clean, dry bowl until soft peaks form. Slowly add the sugar, beating well after each addition until stiff and glossy. Fold in the coconut. Spread into the tin and bake for 20 minutes, or until light brown. While still warm, press down lightly but firmly with a palette knife. Cool completely.

Chop the chocolate into small even-sized pieces and place in a heatproof bowl. Bring a saucepan of water to the boil, then remove from the heat. Sit the bowl over the pan — ensure the bowl doesn't touch the water. Stand, stirring occasionally, until the chocolate has melted. Cool slightly.

Beat the cream until thick. Gently fold in the chocolate until well combined — do not overmix or it will curdle. Spread evenly over the base and refrigerate for 3 hours, or until set. Lift from the tin and dust with the cocoa.

Makes 24 pieces

Gingerbread apricot upside-down cake

200 g (³/₄ cup) glacé apricots
175 g unsalted butter
30 g (¹/₃ cup) pecan nuts, finely
  chopped
165 g (³/₄ cup) firmly packed soft
  brown sugar
90 g (¹/₄ cup) golden syrup
185 g (1¹/₂ cups) self-raising flour
3 teaspoons ground ginger
¹/₂ teaspoon ground nutmeg

Preheat the oven to 180°C (350°F/ Gas 4). Grease and flour the base of a deep 20 cm round cake tin, shaking out the excess flour.

Arrange the apricots around the base of the tin, cut-side-up. Melt the butter in a small saucepan over low heat. Transfer 1 tablespoon of the melted butter to a small bowl. Add the pecans and 55 g (¹/₄ cup) of the brown sugar and mix well. Sprinkle the mixture over the apricots.

Add the golden syrup and 125 ml (¹/₂ cup) water to the saucepan of melted butter and stir over medium heat until well combined. Sift the flour and spices in a bowl, then stir in the remaining sugar. Pour in the golden syrup mixture and mix well. Spoon the mixture over the apricots and smooth the surface.

Bake for 35–40 minutes, or until a skewer comes out clean when inserted into the centre of the cake. Leave in the tin for 15 minutes before turning out onto a wire rack to cool. If desired, serve with custard.

Serves 6

Storage: This cake keeps for 4 days in an airtight cake tin.

Walnut brownies

85 g (2/3 cup) self-raising flour
85 g (2/3 cup) cocoa powder
250 g (1 cup) caster sugar
330 g unsalted butter, melted
4 eggs, lightly beaten
1 teaspoon vanilla essence
250 g (1½ cups) dark chocolate
  bits (chocolate chips)
125 g (1 cup) walnut pieces
icing sugar, to dust

Preheat the oven to 180°C (350°F/ Gas 4). Grease a 20 x 30 cm shallow baking tin and line with baking paper, leaving it hanging over the two long sides of the tin.

Sift together the flour and cocoa, then add the sugar. Make a well in the centre, then add the butter, eggs and vanilla and beat until smooth. Fold in the chocolate bits and walnuts.

Spoon into the tin and smooth the surface. Bake for 25 minutes, or until a skewer comes out clean. Leave in the tin for 10 minutes, then turn onto a wire rack to cool. Dust with icing sugar.

Makes 24 pieces

Devil's food cake

165 g (1 ⅓ cups) plain flour
85 g (⅔ cup) cocoa powder
1 teaspoon bicarbonate of soda
250 g (1 cup) sugar
250 ml (1 cup) buttermilk
2 eggs, lightly beaten
125 g unsalted butter, softened
125 ml (½ cup) whipping cream
icing sugar, to dust
fresh berries, to garnish

Preheat the oven to 180°C (350°F/ Gas 4). Grease a deep 20 cm round cake tin and line the base with baking paper. Sift the flour, cocoa and bicarbonate of soda into a large bowl.

Add the sugar to the sifted dry ingredients. Combine the buttermilk, eggs and butter, then pour onto the dry ingredients. Beat with electric beaters on low speed for 3 minutes, or until just combined. Increase the speed to high and beat for 3 minutes, or until the mixture is free of lumps and increased in volume. Spoon the mixture into the prepared tin and smooth the surface.

Bake for 40–50 minutes, or until a skewer comes out clean when inserted into the centre of the cake. Leave in the tin for 15 minutes before turning out onto a wire rack to cool completely. Cut the cake in half horizontally and fill with whipped cream. Dust with icing sugar and garnish with fresh berries.

Serves 8

Storage: Unfilled, the cake will keep for 3 days in an airtight container or up to 3 months in the freezer. The filled cake is best assembled and eaten on the day of baking.

Apple shortcake

250 g (2 cups) plain flour
1 teaspoon baking powder
125 g unsalted butter, chilled and
   chopped
60 g (¼ cup) caster sugar
1 egg, lightly beaten
1 tablespoon cold milk
4 small red apples, peeled, quartered
   and cored
1 teaspoon ground cinnamon
2 tablespoons caster sugar, extra
1 tablespoon milk, extra
demerara sugar, to sprinkle

Preheat the oven to 180°C (350°F/ Gas 4). Lightly grease a baking tray and line with baking paper, leaving it hanging over the two long sides.

Sift the flour and baking powder into a large bowl, add the butter and rub with your fingers until the mixture resembles fine breadcrumbs. Stir in the sugar.

Make a well in the centre and add the combined egg and milk. Mix with a flat-bladed knife using a cutting action until the mixture comes together in beads. Gently gather together and lift out onto a lightly floured work surface. Press together into a ball, flatten slightly, cover in plastic wrap and chill for 20–30 minutes.

Halve the dough — keep one half in the refrigerator and roll the other half into an even 20 cm square. Put on the baking tray. Cut the apple quarters into thin slices and arrange in rows, to form a double layer of apples over the pastry. Sprinkle with the cinnamon and extra caster sugar.

Roll the remaining pastry into a 20 cm square and put over the apple. Brush with milk and sprinkle with demerara sugar. Bake for 40–45 minutes, or until crisp and golden.

Makes 9 pieces

Panforte

110 g (³/₄ cup) hazelnuts
110 g (³/₄ cup) almonds
125 g (²/₃ cup) candied mixed peel, chopped
100 g (²/₃ cup) candied pineapple, chopped
grated zest of 1 lemon
75 g (²/₃ cup) plain flour
1 teaspoon ground cinnamon
¼ teaspoon ground coriander
¼ teaspoon ground cloves
¼ teaspoon grated nutmeg
pinch of white pepper
150 g (²/₃ cup) sugar
4 tablespoons honey
50 g unsalted butter
icing sugar, to dust

Line a 20 cm springform tin with rice paper or baking paper and grease well with butter.

Toast the nuts under a hot grill, turning them so they brown on all sides, then leave to cool. Put the nuts in a bowl with the mixed peel, pineapple, lemon zest, flour and spices and toss together. Preheat the oven to 150°C (300°F/Gas 2).

Put the sugar, honey and butter in a saucepan and melt them together. Cook the syrup until it reaches 118°C (245°F) on a sugar thermometer, or a little of it dropped into cold water forms a firm ball when moulded between your fingers (see page 393).

Pour the syrup into the nut mixture and mix well, working fast before it stiffens too much. Pour straight into the prepared tin, smooth the surface and bake for 35 minutes. (Unlike other cakes, this cake will neither firm up as it cooks nor colour at all, so you need to time it carefully.)

Cool in the tin until the cake firms up enough to remove the side of the tin. Peel off the paper and leave to cool completely. Dust the top with icing sugar.

Serves 10

Pumpkin fruitcake

250 g pumpkin, peeled and cut into
    small pieces
125 g unsalted butter, softened
140 g (³/₄ cup) soft brown sugar
2 tablespoons golden syrup
2 eggs, lightly beaten
250 g (2 cups) self-raising flour, sifted
200 g (1 cup) mixed dried fruit
2 tablespoons chopped glacé ginger

Preheat the oven to 150°C (300°F/ Gas 2). Grease a deep 20 cm round cake tin and line the base and side with baking paper.

Steam the pumpkin for 10 minutes, or until cooked through. Mash with a potato masher or a fork until smooth. Measure 200 g (³/₄ cup) and set aside until ready to use.

Beat the butter and sugar together with electric beaters until pale and creamy. Add the golden syrup and beat well. Gradually add the egg, beating well after each addition. Fold in the pumpkin until combined. Combine the flour, dried fruit and ginger, then fold into the butter mixture with a metal spoon until combined. Spoon the mixture into the prepared tin and smooth the surface.

Bake for 1 hour 40 minutes, or until a skewer comes out clean when inserted into the centre of the cake. Cool in the tin for 20 minutes before turning out onto a wire rack.

Serves 8–10

Snickerdoodle slice

250 g (2 cups) plain flour
250 g (1 cup) caster sugar
1 tablespoon ground cinnamon
2 teaspoons baking powder
2 eggs
250 ml (1 cup) milk
125 g unsalted butter, melted
3 tablespoons sugar
3 teaspoons ground cinnamon, extra

Preheat the oven to 180°C (350°F/ Gas 4). Lightly grease a 20 x 30 cm baking tin and line with baking paper, hanging over the two long sides.

Sift together the flour, caster sugar, cinnamon and baking powder and make a well in the centre. In a small bowl, whisk together the eggs and milk. Pour into the flour and mix with a metal spoon to roughly combine. Fold in the butter until smooth — do not overmix. Spoon half the mixture into the tin and level the surface.

Combine the sugar and extra cinnamon, and sprinkle two-thirds over the mixture in the tin. Gently spoon the remaining mixture over the top, then sprinkle the remaining cinnamon sugar over the surface. Bake for 25–30 minutes, or until firm. Cool in the tin for 20 minutes, then lift onto a wire rack to cool.

Makes 20 pieces

Carrot, spice and sour cream cake

310 g (2½ cups) self-raising flour
2 teaspoons ground cinnamon
1 teaspoon ground nutmeg
150 g (¾ cup) dark brown sugar
200 g (1⅓ cups) grated carrot (about
   260 g carrots)
4 eggs
250 g (1 cup) sour cream
250 ml (1 cup) vegetable oil

Orange cream cheese frosting
60 g (¼ cup) cream cheese, softened
20 g unsalted butter, softened
1 teaspoon grated orange zest
2 teaspoons orange juice
125 g (1 cup) icing sugar

Preheat the oven to 160°C (315°F/ Gas 2–3). Grease a deep 22 cm round tin and line the base with baking paper. Sift the flour and spices into a large bowl, then stir in the brown sugar and grated carrot until well mixed.

Combine the eggs, sour cream and oil until lightly beaten. Add to the carrot mixture and stir until well combined. Spoon the mixture into the prepared tin and smooth the surface.

Bake for 1 hour 15 minutes, or until a skewer comes out clean when inserted into the centre of the cake. Leave in the tin for 10 minutes before turning out onto a wire rack to cool.

To make the frosting, beat the cream cheese, butter, zest and juice in a bowl with electric beaters until light and fluffy. Gradually beat in the icing sugar until smooth. Spread over the cooled cake.

Serves 8–10

Mini mango cakes with lime syrup

425 g tin mango slices in syrup, drained
90 g unsalted butter, softened
185 g ($3/4$ cup) caster sugar
2 eggs, lightly beaten
60 g ($1/2$ cup) self-raising flour
2 tablespoons ground almonds
2 tablespoons coconut milk
2 tablespoons lime juice

Preheat the oven to 200°C (400°F/ Gas 6). Grease four 250 ml (1 cup) muffin holes and line with mango slices. Beat the butter and 125 g ($1/2$ cup) of the sugar in a bowl with electric beaters until light and creamy. Gradually add the egg, beating well after each addition. Fold in the sifted flour, then add the almonds and coconut milk, then spoon into the muffin holes. Bake for 25 minutes, or until a skewer comes out clean when inserted into the centre of the cakes.

To make the syrup, place the lime juice, the remaining sugar and 125 ml ($1/2$ cup) water in a small saucepan and stir over low heat until the sugar dissolves. Increase the heat and simmer for 10 minutes. Pierce holes in each cake with a skewer. Drizzle the syrup over the top and allow to stand for 5 minutes to soak up the liquid. Turn out and serve.

Makes 4

Apple and berry crumble muffins

155 g (1¼ cups) self-raising flour
150 g (1 cup) wholemeal self-raising
  flour
¼ teaspoon ground cinnamon
pinch ground cloves
115 g (½ cup) firmly packed soft
  brown sugar
185 ml (¾ cup) milk
2 eggs
125 g unsalted butter, melted
  and cooled
2 Granny Smith apples, peeled,
  cored, grated
155 g (1 cup) blueberries

Crumble
5 tablespoons plain flour
55 g (¼ cup) demerara sugar
35 g (⅓ cup) rolled oats
40 g unsalted butter, chopped

Preheat the oven to 190°C (375°F/
Gas 5). Line 12 regular muffin holes
with muffin papers. Sift the flours,
cinnamon and cloves into a large
bowl, add the husks and stir in the
sugar. Make a well in the centre.

Put the milk, eggs and butter in a jug,
whisk and pour into the well. Fold
gently until just combined — the
batter should be lumpy. Fold in the
fruit. Divide among the muffin holes.

To make the crumble, put the flour,
sugar and oats in a bowl. Rub the
butter in with your fingertips until
most of the lumps are gone. Sprinkle
2 teaspoons of the crumble over each
muffin. Bake for 25 minutes, or until
golden. Cool for 5 minutes, then
transfer to a wire rack.

Makes 12 regular muffins

Apricot and raisin bran loaf

150 g (³/₄ cup) dried apricots,
  chopped
160 g (1 cup) raisins
70 g (1 cup) processed bran cereal
95 g (½ cup) soft brown sugar
375 ml (1½ cups) warm milk
125 g (1 cup) self-raising flour, sifted
75 g (½ cup) wholemeal self-raising
  flour, sifted
1 teaspoon mixed spice

Preheat the oven to 180°C (350°F/ Gas 4). Grease a deep 18.5 x 11 cm loaf tin and line the base and sides with baking paper.

Soak the apricots, raisins, bran cereal and brown sugar in the milk in a large bowl for 30 minutes, or until the milk is almost completely absorbed. Stir in the flours and mixed spice to form a stiff moist batter. Spoon the mixture into the tin and smooth the surface.

Bake for 50 minutes, or until a skewer comes out clean when inserted into the centre of the cake — cover with foil during cooking if it browns too much. Leave in the tin for 10 minutes, then turn out onto a wire rack to cool. Cut into thick slices. If desired, serve with butter and dust with icing sugar.

Serves 6–8

Note: Use any dried fruit combination. This loaf is delicious toasted.

Berry and apple slice

150 g unsalted butter
320 g (1⅓ cups) caster sugar
2 eggs, lightly beaten
250 g (2 cups) self-raising flour, sifted
160 ml (⅔ cup) buttermilk
1 teaspoon vanilla essence
2 large apples
150 g (1 cup) blueberries
150 g (1¼ cups) blackberries
icing sugar, to dust

Preheat the oven to 180°C (350°F/ Gas 4). Lightly grease a 30 x 20 cm shallow baking tin and line with baking paper, leaving it hanging over the two long sides.

Beat the butter and sugar with electric beaters until light and fluffy. Add the egg gradually, beating well after each addition. Stir in the flour and buttermilk alternately and mix until smooth. Stir through the vanilla. Spread a 5 mm layer of mixture over the base of the tin.

Peel, quarter and core the apples. Cut into very thin slices and arrange on the mixture. Spoon the remaining mixture over the apple and smooth the surface, then scatter with the blueberries and blackberries. Bake on the middle rack for 40 minutes, or until cooked and golden.

Cool in the tin for 30 minutes before lifting onto a wire rack. When completely cooled, dust with icing sugar and cut into squares.

Makes 12 pieces

Walnut cake with chocolate icing

185 g unsalted butter, softened
95 g (1/2 cup) soft brown sugar
2 eggs
185 g (1 1/2 cups) self-raising flour
90 g (3/4 cup) chopped walnuts
60 ml (1/4 cup) milk

Chocolate icing
125 g good-quality dark chocolate, chopped
20 g unsalted butter

Preheat the oven to 180°C (350°F/ Gas 4). Grease a 20 cm springform tin and line the base with baking paper.

Place the butter and sugar in a large bowl. Beat with electric beaters for 5 minutes, or until thick and creamy. Add the eggs one at a time, beating well after each addition. Fold in the flour and 60 g (1/2 cup) of the walnuts alternately with the milk until just combined. Spoon the mixture into the prepared tin and smooth the surface.

Bake for 35 minutes, or until a skewer comes out clean when inserted into the centre of the cake. Leave in the tin for 5 minutes before turning out onto a wire rack to cool.

To make the chocolate icing, put the chocolate and butter in a heatproof bowl. Bring a saucepan of water to the boil, then reduce the heat to a gentle simmer. Sit the bowl over the saucepan, making sure the base of the bowl does not touch the water. Stir occasionally to ensure even melting. Cool slightly, then spread over the cake. Sprinkle with the remaining walnuts.

Serves 6

Florentines

55 g unsalted butter
45 g (¼ cup) soft brown sugar
2 teaspoons honey
25 g (¼ cup) flaked almonds, roughly
  chopped
2 tablespoons chopped dried apricots
2 tablespoons chopped glacé
  cherries
2 tablespoons mixed peel
40 g (⅓ cup) plain flour, sifted
120 g dark chocolate

Preheat the oven to 180°C (350°F/ Gas 4). Melt the butter, brown sugar and honey in a pan until the butter is melted and all the ingredients are combined. Remove from the heat and add the almonds, apricots, glacé cherries, mixed peel and the flour. Mix well.

Grease and line two baking trays with baking paper. Place level tablespoons of the mixture well apart on the trays. Reshape and flatten the biscuits into 5 cm rounds before cooking.

Bake for 10 minutes, or until lightly browned. Cool on the tray, then allow to cool completely on a wire rack.

To melt the chocolate, break it up into small pieces and put it in a heatproof bowl. Bring a pan of water to a simmer, remove from the heat and place the bowl over the pan. Stir the chocolate until melted. Spread the melted chocolate on the bottom of each florentine and, using a fork, make a wavy pattern on the chocolate before it sets. Let the chocolate set before serving.

Makes 12

Lemon semolina cake

6 eggs, separated
310 g (1¼ cups) caster sugar
2 teaspoons finely grated lemon zest
80 ml (⅓ cup) lemon juice
90 g (¾ cup) semolina
95 g (1 cup) ground almonds
2 tablespoons self-raising flour
thick (double) cream, to serve

Preheat the oven to 170°C (325°F/ Gas 3). Grease a 24 cm springform tin and line the base with baking paper. Place the egg yolks, 250 g (1 cup) of the sugar, the lemon zest and 2 tablespoons of the lemon juice in a large bowl. Beat with electric beaters for 8 minutes, or until thick and pale and the mixture leaves a trail when the beaters are lifted.

Beat the egg whites in a clean bowl with clean electric beaters until firm peaks form. Gently fold the whites into the egg yolk mixture alternately with the combined semolina, ground almonds and flour — do not overmix or the mixture will deflate. Carefully pour into the prepared tin and smooth the surface. Bake for 35–40 minutes, or until a skewer comes out clean when inserted into the centre of the cake. Leave for 5 minutes in the tin, then turn out onto a wire rack. Pierce a few holes in the cake with a skewer.

Place the remaining lemon juice and sugar in a small saucepan with 125 ml (½ cup) water. Stir over low heat until the sugar has dissolved. Increase the heat and simmer for 3 minutes, or until thick and syrupy. Pour the hot syrup over the cooled cake. Serve with thick cream.

Serves 8–10

Sesame and ginger slice

125 g (1 cup) plain flour
1/2 teaspoon bicarbonate of soda
1 teaspoon ground ginger
1/4 teaspoon mixed spice
2 eggs
140 g (3/4 cup) soft brown sugar
125 g unsalted butter, melted
55 g (1/4 cup) chopped crystallized
   ginger
50 g (1/3 cup) sesame seeds, toasted

Preheat the oven to 180°C (350°F/
Gas 4). Lightly grease a 20 x 30 cm
shallow baking tin and line with
baking paper, leaving it hanging over
the two long sides.

Sift together the flour, bicarbonate
of soda, ginger, mixed spice and
1/4 teaspoon salt. Beat the eggs
and brown sugar in a large bowl for
2 minutes, or until thick and creamy.
Mix in the melted butter and gently
fold in the flour mixture. Add the
crystallized ginger and half the
sesame seeds and mix gently.

Spread into the tin and sprinkle evenly
with the remaining sesame seeds.
Bake for 20 minutes, or until firm to
touch and slightly coloured. Cool in
the tin for 10 minutes, then cool on a
wire rack.

Makes 15 pieces

Chocolate, almond and mixed peel cake

1 tablespoon mixed peel, chopped
150 g dark chocolate pieces
95 g (1 cup) ground almonds
60 g (½ cup) self-raising flour
4 eggs, separated
125 g (½ cup) caster sugar
2 tablespoons warm milk
170 ml (⅔ cup) whipping cream

Preheat the oven to 180°C (350°F/ Gas 4). Grease a 20 cm springform tin and line the base with baking paper. Combine the mixed peel and 100 g of the chocolate in a food processor until finely ground. Add the ground almonds and flour and process briefly to combine.

Beat the egg yolks and sugar with electric beaters for 5 minutes, or until thick and pale — the beaters should leave a trail in the mixture. Stir in the chocolate and peel mixture, then the milk. Beat the egg whites in a clean bowl until soft peaks form. Gently fold the whites into the cake mixture with a metal spoon — do not overmix or it will lose volume. Pour the mixture into the tin and smooth the surface. Bake for 45 minutes, or until a skewer comes out clean when inserted into the centre of the cake. Leave in the tin for 5 minutes, then turn out onto a wire rack to cool.

To make the filling, melt the remaining chocolate pieces in a heatproof bowl over a saucepan of hot water. Cut the cake in half horizontally. Spread the bottom layer with melted chocolate, then the whipped cream. Cover with the remaining layer and, if desired, dust with icing sugar in a pattern.

Serves 6

Sticky gingerbread muffins

250 g (2 cups) self-raising flour, sifted
90 g (³/₄ cup) plain flour, sifted
1/2 teaspoon bicarbonate of soda
3 teaspoons ground ginger
1 teaspoon ground cinnamon
1 teaspoon mixed spice
230 g (1 cup) firmly packed soft
   brown sugar
55 g (¹/₄ cup) chopped glacé ginger
235 g (²/₃ cup) golden syrup
100 g unsalted butter, chopped
250 ml (1 cup) buttermilk
1 egg, lightly beaten
50 g dark chocolate, chopped into
   even-sized pieces, melted (see
   page 390)

Ginger frosting
60 g unsalted butter, softened
1¹/₂ tablespoons golden syrup
125 g (1 cup) icing sugar
1/2 teaspoon ground ginger

Preheat the oven to 200°C (400°F/ Gas 6). Grease 12 regular muffin holes. Put the flours, bicarbonate of soda, ginger, cinnamon and mixed spice into a large bowl and stir in the brown sugar and glacé ginger. Make a well in the centre. Melt the golden syrup and butter in a pan, stirring until well mixed. Cool. Combine the golden syrup mixture, buttermilk and egg in a large jug, mix together and pour into the well. Fold until just combined — the batter will be lumpy.

Divide the mixture among the muffin holes. Bake for 20–25 minutes, or until the muffins come away from the side of the tin. Cool for 5 minutes in the tin, then transfer to a wire rack.

To make the ginger frosting, beat the butter, golden syrup, icing sugar and ground ginger together with electric beaters in a bowl until light and fluffy. Spread over the top of the muffins.

Spoon the melted chocolate into the corner of a plastic bag. Snip off the corner to create a nozzle. Pipe the chocolate over the icing in crisscrossing lines. Apply even pressure and move at a steady speed to prevent the chocolate from clumping. Allow to set before serving.

Makes 12 muffins

Bakewell slice

125 g (1 cup) plain flour
30 g (¼ cup) icing sugar
170 g unsalted butter, chilled
  and chopped
1 egg yolk
125 g (½ cup) caster sugar
4 eggs
125 g (1¼ cups) ground almonds
2 drops almond essence
160 g (½ cup) raspberry jam
25 g (¼ cup) flaked almonds

Preheat the oven to 180°C (350°F/ Gas 4). Lightly grease a 20 x 30 cm baking tin and line with baking paper, hanging over the two long sides.

Sift the flour and 1 tablespoon of the icing sugar into a bowl, add 50 g of the butter and rub it in until the mixture resembles breadcrumbs. Add the egg yolk and 2 tablespoons cold water and mix with a flat-bladed knife until the mixture comes together in beads. Gather into a ball, cover with plastic wrap and refrigerate for 30 minutes. Roll out between two sheets of baking paper, remove the paper and put in the tin, pressing into the edges. Bake for 10 minutes. Cool.

Beat the remaining butter and the caster sugar with electric beaters until creamy. Add the eggs and fold in the ground almonds and almond essence. Spread the jam over the pastry base and pour over the filling. Sprinkle with almonds and bake for 30–35 minutes, or until firm. Allow to cool.

Sift the remaining icing sugar into a bowl and mix in 2–3 teaspoons warm water to form a free-flowing paste. Drizzle over the slice in a zigzag pattern and leave to set. Trim the edges and cut into squares.

Makes 15 pieces

Orange poppy seed cake with citrus icing

50 g (1/3 cup) poppy seeds
185 ml (3/4 cup) warm milk
250 g (1 cup) caster sugar
3 eggs
250 g (2 cups) self-raising flour, sifted
210 g unsalted butter, softened
1 1/2 tablespoons finely grated orange
  zest
250 g (2 cups) icing sugar
thick (double) cream, to serve

Preheat the oven to 180°C (350°F/ Gas 4). Lightly grease a 23 cm fluted baba tin. Combine the poppy seeds and milk in a bowl and set aside for at least 15 minutes.

Place the caster sugar, eggs, flour, 185 g of the butter and 3 teaspoons of the orange zest in a large bowl. Add the poppy seed mixture and beat with electric beaters on low speed until combined. Increase to medium speed and beat for 3 minutes, or until the mixture is thick and pale. Pour the mixture evenly into the prepared tin.

Bake for 50 minutes, or until a skewer comes out clean when inserted into the centre of the cake. Leave in the tin for 5 minutes, then turn out onto a wire rack.

To make the icing, melt the remaining butter, then place the butter in a bowl with the icing sugar, remaining orange zest and 3 tablespoons boiling water. Mix to make a soft icing, then spread over the warm cake and serve with thick cream.

Serves 8

Passionfruit and coconut cheese slice

100 g (¾ cup) slivered almonds
125 g (1 cup) plain flour
1 teaspoon baking powder
100 g unsalted butter, chopped
125 g (½ cup) caster sugar
1 egg yolk
25 g (¼ cup) desiccated coconut
750 g (3 cups) cream cheese, softened
2 eggs
185 ml (¾ cup) coconut milk
3 teaspoons vanilla essence
½ teaspoon lemon juice
185 g (¾ cup) caster sugar, extra
65 g (¾ cup) flaked almonds, toasted (see page 390)

Topping
90 g (¾ cup) icing sugar
40 g unsalted butter, softened
1 tablespoon cornflour
2 tablespoons strained passionfruit juice

Finely chop the almonds in a food processor. Sift the flour and baking powder into a bowl. Rub the butter into the flour until it resembles breadcrumbs. Stir in the almonds and sugar. Make a well in the centre and add the egg yolk. Mix with a flat-bladed knife until the mixture comes together in beads. Remove to a lightly floured work surface and shape into a ball. Flatten slightly, cover in plastic wrap and refrigerate for 30 minutes.

Preheat the oven to 170°C (325°F/ Gas 3). Grease a 30 x 20 x 5 cm tin and line with baking paper, hanging over the two long sides. Roll the dough out to fit the tin and press in evenly. Sprinkle over the coconut and lightly press it in. Bake for 10 minutes and cool for 10 minutes. Combine the cream cheese and eggs in the food processor. Add coconut milk, vanilla, lemon juice and the extra sugar, and blend until smooth. Pour over the base. Bake for 40 minutes. Cool in the tin.

To make the topping, mix the icing sugar and butter with a wooden spoon until smooth. Stir in the cornflour, then the passionfruit juice. Mix until smooth, then spread over the slice. Scatter over the toasted almonds. Leave to set, then cut into 5 cm squares.

Makes 24 pieces

Pecan and coffee biscotti

215 g (1³/₄ cups) plain flour
¹/₂ teaspoon baking powder
160 g (²/₃ cup) caster sugar
60 g unsalted butter
2 eggs
¹/₂ teaspoon vanilla essence
2 tablespoons instant coffee granules
135 g (1¹/₃ cups) pecan nuts
¹/₂ teaspoon caster sugar, extra

Preheat the oven to 180°C (350°F/ Gas 4) and line two baking trays with baking paper. Put the sifted flour, baking powder, sugar and a pinch of salt in a food processor and mix for 1–2 seconds. Add the butter and mix until the mixture resembles fine breadcrumbs. Add the eggs and vanilla and process until smooth.

Transfer the dough to a well-floured surface and knead in the coffee and pecans. Divide into two equal portions and, using lightly floured hands, shape each into a log about 20 cm long. Place the logs on the baking trays and sprinkle with the extra sugar. Press the top of each log down gently to make an oval.

Bake for 35 minutes, or until golden. Remove and set aside to cool for about 20 minutes. Reduce the oven temperature to 170°C (325°F/Gas 3).

Cut the logs into 1 cm slices. Turn the baking paper over, then spread the biscotti well apart on the tray so that they do not touch. Return to the oven and bake for 30 minutes, or until they just begin to colour. Cool completely before storing in an airtight container.

Makes 40

Caramel peach cake

250 g unsalted butter, softened
60 g (⅓ cup) soft brown sugar
825 g tin peach halves in natural juice
250 g (1 cup) caster sugar
3 teaspoons finely grated lemon zest
3 eggs, lightly beaten
310 g (2½ cups) self-raising flour,
  sifted
250 g (1 cup) plain yoghurt

Preheat the oven to 180°C (350°F/ Gas 4). Grease a deep 23 cm round cake tin and line the base with baking paper. Melt 50 g of the butter and pour on the base of the tin. Evenly sprinkle the brown sugar over the top. Drain the peaches, reserving 1 tablespoon of the liquid. Arrange the peach halves, cut-side-up, over the sugar mixture.

Beat the caster sugar, lemon zest and remaining butter with electric beaters for 5–6 minutes, or until pale and creamy. Add the egg gradually, beating well after each addition — the mixture may look curdled but once you add the flour, it will bring it back together. Using a metal spoon, fold in the flour alternately with the yoghurt (in two batches), then the reserved peach liquid. Spoon the mixture over the peaches and smooth the surface.

Bake for 1 hour 25 minutes, or until a skewer comes out clean when inserted into the centre of the cake. Cool in the tin for 30 minutes before turning out onto a large serving plate.

Serves 10–12

Orange, pistachio and semolina slice

100 g (²/₃ cup) shelled pistachio nuts
200 g unsalted butter, chopped
160 g (²/₃ cup) caster sugar
1 teaspoon vanilla essence
1 tablespoon finely grated orange zest
2 eggs
60 g (½ cup) self-raising flour, sifted
125 ml (½ cup) orange juice
185 g (1½ cups) fine semolina
250 g (1 cup) caster sugar, extra
125 ml (½ cup) orange juice, extra
icing sugar, to dust

Preheat the oven to 180°C (350°F/ Gas 4). Lightly grease a 20 x 30 cm shallow baking tin and line with baking paper, leaving it hanging over on the two long sides.

Bake the pistachios for 8–10 minutes, or until they are lightly toasted. Cool, then chop.

Beat the butter and sugar with electric beaters until light and fluffy. Add the vanilla, orange zest and eggs, and beat until combined.

Add the flour, orange juice, semolina and pistachio nuts, and fold in with a spatula until just combined — do not overmix. Spread into the tin. Bake for 30 minutes, or until golden brown and firm when lightly touched. Cool for 10 minutes in the tin, then on a wire rack placed on a tray.

Mix the extra sugar and orange juice in a small saucepan. Bring to the boil over medium heat, then simmer for 1 minute. Spoon over the slice. Cool and cut into squares or diamonds. Dust with icing sugar.

Makes 18 pieces

Raisin butter cake

160 g (1 cup) raisins
60 ml (¼ cup) rum
1 tablespoon soft brown sugar
250 g unsalted butter, softened
230 g (1 cup) firmly packed soft
  brown sugar, extra
3 eggs, lightly beaten
310 g (2½ cups) self-raising flour,
  sifted
185 ml (¾ cup) buttermilk

Coffee buttercream
3 teaspoons instant coffee powder
125 g unsalted butter, softened
185 g (1½ cups) icing sugar, sifted
½ teaspoon vanilla essence
2 teaspoons milk

Preheat the oven to 180°C (350°F/ Gas 4). Lightly grease a 23 cm round cake tin and line the base with baking paper. Combine the raisins, rum and brown sugar in a small saucepan. Bring to the boil, reduce the heat and simmer for 30 seconds, or until the rum is absorbed. Set aside to cool.

Beat the butter and extra brown sugar with electric beaters until pale and creamy. Add the egg gradually, beating well after each addition — the mixture may look curdled but once you add the flour, it will bring it back together. Using a metal spoon, fold in the flour and buttermilk in two batches, then fold in the raisin and rum mixture.

Spoon the mixture into the tin and bake for 1 hour 30 minutes, or until a skewer comes out clean when inserted into the centre of the cake. Leave in the tin for 10 minutes before turning it out onto a wire rack to cool.

To make the buttercream, dissolve the coffee in 2 tablespoons boiling water. Beat the butter and icing sugar with electric beaters until pale and creamy. Add the vanilla, coffee mixture and milk and beat for 2 minutes, or until smooth and fluffy. Spread over the cool cake.

Serves 10

Passionfruit melting moments

250 g unsalted butter
40 g (⅓ cup) icing sugar
1 teaspoon vanilla essence
185 g (1½ cups) self-raising flour
60 g (½ cup) custard powder

Passionfruit filling
60 g unsalted butter
60 g (½ cup) icing sugar
1½ tablespoons passionfruit pulp

Preheat the oven to 180°C (350°F/ Gas 4). Line two baking trays with baking paper. Beat the butter and sugar until light and creamy. Beat in the vanilla essence. Sift in the flour and custard powder and mix to a soft dough. Roll level tablespoons of the mixture into 28 balls and place on the trays. Flatten slightly with a floured fork.

Bake for 20 minutes, or until lightly golden. Cool on a wire rack.

To make the filling, beat the butter and sugar until light and creamy, then beat in the passionfruit pulp. Use the filling to sandwich the biscuits together. Leave to firm before serving.

Makes 14 filled biscuits

Variation: You can vary the flavour of the filling. To make a coffee filling, for example, dissolve 2 teaspoons of instant coffee in 2 teaspoons water and add to the butter and sugar mixture. Beat until well combined.

Apricot pine nut cake

100 g (²/₃ cup) pine nuts, roughly
  chopped
250 g unsalted butter, softened
250 g (1 cup) sugar
3 teaspoons finely grated orange zest
3 eggs, lightly beaten
310 g (2½ cups) self-raising flour,
  sifted
200 g (³/₄ cup) glacé apricots, finely
  chopped
250 ml (1 cup) orange juice

Preheat the oven to 180°C (350°F/ Gas 4). Lightly grease a 26 cm round cake tin and line the base with baking paper. Spread the pine nuts on a baking tray and bake for 5–10 minutes, or until lightly golden. Leave to cool.

Beat the butter, sugar and orange zest with electric beaters until pale and creamy. Add the egg gradually, beating well after each addition — the mixture may look curdled but once you add the flour, it will bring it back together. Fold in the sifted flour, pine nuts, apricots and orange juice in two batches with a metal spoon. Spoon the mixture into the prepared tin and smooth the surface.

Bake for 1 hour 20 minutes, or until a skewer comes out clean when inserted into the centre of the cake. Leave in the tin for 10 minutes before turning onto a wire rack to cool. If desired, dust with icing sugar and serve with cream or yoghurt.

Serves 10

Note: The chopped apricots may clump together, so flour your hands and rub through to separate.
Variation: For a little extra flavour, add 2 tablespoons brandy to the cake mixture with the flour, pine nuts, apricots and orange juice.

Quick banana bread

250 g (1 cup) cream cheese, softened
220 g (1 cup) raw sugar
3 large ripe bananas, mashed (about
1 cup)
2 eggs, lightly beaten
300 g packet scone mix
60 g (½ cup) chopped pecan nuts

Preheat the oven to 180°C (350°F/ Gas 4). Grease a 22 x 12 cm loaf tin and line the base and two long sides with a long sheet of baking paper.

Beat the cream cheese and sugar in a large bowl with electric beaters until light and smooth. Add the banana and eggs and beat for 2 minutes, or until well combined. Fold in the scone mix and pecans until well combined.

Spoon the mixture into the prepared tin and smooth the surface. Bake for 40 minutes. Cover with foil and bake for a further 15 minutes, or until a skewer comes out clean when inserted into the centre of the cake. Leave in the tin for 10 minutes before turning out onto a wire rack to cool. Cool completely before serving.

Serves 12

Note: This banana bread may be served with or without butter. It will keep well for up to 5 days stored in an airtight container.

Chewy fruit and seed slice

200 g unsalted butter
175 g (½ cup) golden syrup
125 g (½ cup) crunchy peanut butter
2 teaspoons vanilla essence
30 g (¼ cup) plain flour
30 g (⅓ cup) ground almonds
½ teaspoon mixed spice
300 g (3 cups) quick-cooking oats
2 teaspoons finely grated orange zest
185 g (1 cup) soft brown sugar
45 g (½ cup) desiccated coconut
50 g (⅓ cup) sesame seeds, toasted
90 g (½ cup) pepitas or shelled
   sunflower seeds
80 g (½ cup) raisins, chopped
45 g (¼ cup) mixed peel

Preheat the oven to 170°C (325°F/ Gas 3). Lightly grease a 20 x 30 cm shallow tin and line with baking paper, leaving it hanging over the two long sides.

Place the butter and golden syrup in a small saucepan over low heat, stirring occasionally until melted. Remove from the heat and stir in the peanut butter and vanilla until combined.

Mix together the remaining ingredients, stirring well. Make a well in the centre and add the butter and syrup mixture. Mix with a large metal spoon until combined. Press evenly into the tin and bake for 25 minutes, or until golden and firm. Cool in the tin, then cut into squares.

Makes 18 pieces

Rich dark chocolate cake

185 g unsalted butter, chopped
250 g (1½ cups) dark chocolate
  bits (chocolate chips)
215 g (1¾ cups) self-raising flour
40 g (⅓ cup) cocoa powder
375 g (1½ cups) caster sugar
3 eggs, lightly beaten

Chocolate topping
20 g unsalted butter, chopped
125 g dark chocolate, chopped

Preheat the oven to 160°C (315°F/ Gas 2–3). Grease a 22 cm springform tin and line the base with baking paper. Place the butter and chocolate bits in a small heatproof bowl and melt, stirring frequently, over a saucepan of simmering water. Make sure the base of the bowl doesn't touch the water.

Sift the flour and cocoa into a large bowl. Combine the melted butter and chocolate mixture, sugar and egg, then add 250 ml (1 cup) water and mix well. Add to the flour and cocoa and stir until well combined.

Pour the mixture into the prepared tin and bake for 1 hour 30 minutes, or until a skewer comes out clean when inserted into the centre of the cake. Leave in the tin for 15 minutes before turning out onto a wire rack to cool.

To make the chocolate topping, place the butter and chocolate pieces in a small heatproof bowl and melt, stirring frequently, over a saucepan of simmering water — ensure the base of the bowl doesn't touch the water. Spread the topping over the cooled cake in a swirl pattern.

Serves 10–12

Choc chip cookies

125 g unsalted butter
185 g (1 cup) soft brown sugar
1 teaspoon vanilla essence
1 egg, lightly beaten
1 tablespoon milk
215 g (1¾ cups) plain flour
1 teaspoon baking powder
250 g (1½ cups) dark chocolate bits
  (chocolate chips)

Preheat the oven to 180°C (350°F/ Gas 4). Line a large baking tray with baking paper.

Cream the butter and sugar with electric beaters in a large bowl. Mix in the vanilla essence and gradually add the egg, beating well. Stir in the milk. Sift the flour and baking powder into a large bowl, then fold into the butter and egg mixture. Stir in the dark chocolate bits.

Drop level tablespoons of the cookie mixture onto the baking tray, leaving about 4 cm between each cookie, then lightly press with a floured fork. Bake for 15 minutes, or until lightly golden. Cool on a wire rack.

Makes 16

Passionfruit and lemon delicious slice

120 g unsalted butter, softened
60 g (½ cup) icing sugar, sifted
½ teaspoon vanilla essence
185 g (1½ cups) plain flour, sifted
1 teaspoon grated lemon zest
icing sugar, to dust

Filling
100 g (¾ cup) plain flour
½ teaspoon baking powder
65 g (¾ cup) desiccated coconut
3 eggs
250 g (1 cup) caster sugar
170 g tin passionfruit pulp
2 tablespoons lemon juice
1 teaspoon grated lemon zest

Preheat the oven to 180°C (350°F/ Gas 4). Lightly grease an 18 x 27 cm baking tin and line with baking paper, leaving the paper hanging over the two long sides.

Cream the butter and icing sugar with electric beaters until pale and creamy, then add the vanilla. Fold in the flour and lemon zest with a large metal spoon. Press into the tin and bake for 15–20 minutes, or until lightly golden.

To make the filling, sift the flour and baking powder together and add the coconut. Lightly beat the eggs and sugar in a bowl, then add the passionfruit pulp, lemon juice and zest. Add the dry ingredients and stir until combined. Pour over the base and bake for 20 minutes, or until firm to touch. Cool in the tin. Dust with icing sugar and cut into pieces.

Makes 18 pieces

Rum and raisin cake

160 g (1¼ cups) raisins
60 ml (¼ cup) dark rum
185 g (1½ cups) self-raising flour
150 g unsalted butter, chopped
140 g (¾ cup) soft brown sugar
3 eggs, lightly beaten
ice cream, to serve

Preheat the oven to 180°C (350°F/ Gas 4). Grease a deep 20 cm round cake tin and line the base with baking paper. Soak the raisins and rum in a small bowl for 10 minutes. Sift the flour into a large bowl and make a well in the centre.

Melt the butter and sugar in a small saucepan over low heat, stirring until the sugar has dissolved. Remove from the heat. Combine with the rum and raisin mixture and add to the flour with the egg. Stir with a wooden spoon until combined — do not overbeat. Spoon the mixture into the prepared tin and smooth the surface.

Bake for 40 minutes, or until a skewer comes out clean when inserted into the centre of the cake. Delicious served with ice cream.

Serves 8

Glacé fruit slice

480 g (2 cups) roughly chopped glacé
   fruit
2 tablespoons rum
100 g unsalted butter, softened
90 g ($1/3$ cup) caster sugar
2 eggs
2 teaspoons vanilla essence
125 g (1 cup) mixed toasted nuts,
   roughly chopped
30 g ($1/4$ cup) plain flour, sifted
30 g ($1/4$ cup) self-raising flour, sifted
25 g ($1/4$ cup) milk powder
80 g ($2/3$ cup) icing sugar
1 teaspoon rum, extra

Preheat the oven to 190°C (375°F/
Gas 5). Lightly grease an 18 x 27 cm
shallow baking tin and line with
baking paper, hanging over the two
long sides.

Combine the glacé fruit and rum in a
bowl. Beat the butter and sugar with
electric beaters until light and fluffy.
Add the eggs one at a time, beating
well after each addition. Beat in the
vanilla, then stir in the fruit mixture,
nuts, flours and milk powder.

Spread evenly into the tin. Bake for
15 minutes, then reduce the oven to
180°C (350°F/Gas 4) and bake for
10 minutes, or until golden brown.
Cool in the tin until just warm.

Combine the icing sugar, extra rum
and 1 teaspoon water until smooth
and spreadable but not runny. If the
icing is too thick, add a little more rum
or water. Spread over the slice and
cool completely. Cut into three
lengthways strips, then cut each strip
into eight pieces.

Makes 24 pieces

Chocolate hazelnut friands

200 g (1 1/2 cups) hazelnuts
185 g unsalted butter
6 egg whites
155 g (1 1/4 cups) plain flour
30 g (1/4 cup) cocoa powder
250 g (2 cups) icing sugar
icing sugar, extra, to dust

Preheat the oven to 200°C (400°F/ Gas 6). Grease twelve 125 ml (1/2 cup) friand or muffin holes. Spread the hazelnuts out on a baking tray and bake for 8–10 minutes, or until fragrant (take care not to burn). Put in a clean tea towel and rub vigorously to loosen the skins. Discard the skins. Cool, then process in a food processor until finely ground.

Place the butter in a small pan and melt over medium heat, then cook for 3–4 minutes, or until it turns a deep golden colour. Strain any dark solids and set aside to cool (the colour will become deeper on standing).

Lightly whisk the egg whites in a bowl until frothy but not firm. Sift the flour, cocoa powder and icing sugar into a large bowl and stir in the ground hazelnuts. Make a well in the centre, add the egg whites and butter and mix until combined.

Spoon the mixture into the friand holes until three-quarters filled. Bake for 20–25 minutes, or until a skewer inserted into the centre comes out clean. Leave in the tin for a few minutes, then cool on a wire rack. Dust with icing sugar, to serve.

Makes 12

Apple teacake

150 g unsalted butter, chopped
200 g (1 cup) caster sugar
2 eggs, lightly beaten
1 teaspoon vanilla essence
185 g (1½ cups) self-raising flour,
    sifted
185 g (¾ cup) vanilla-flavoured
    yoghurt
1 apple (Granny Smith), peeled, cored
    and thinly sliced
1 teaspoon ground cinnamon

Preheat the oven to 180°C (350°F/ Gas 4). Grease a deep 20 cm round cake tin and line the base with baking paper. Beat 130 g of the butter and 185 g (¾ cup) of the sugar with electric beaters until light and creamy.

Gradually add the egg, beating well after each addition until combined. Add the vanilla essence. Fold in the flour, then the yoghurt and stir until smooth. Spoon the mixture into the prepared tin and smooth the surface.

Arrange the apple slices evenly over the mixture in a circular pattern starting in the centre. Sprinkle with the cinnamon and the remaining sugar. Melt the remaining butter, then drizzle over the top.

Bake for 1 hour, or until a skewer comes out clean when inserted into the centre of the cake. Leave in the tin for 30 minutes before turning out onto a wire rack to cool. If desired, combine a little extra cinnamon and sugar and sprinkle over the apple.

Serves 8

Cider crumble slice

60 g unsalted butter
1½ tablespoons golden syrup
150 ml (⅔ cup) alcoholic apple cider
250 g (2 cups) self-raising flour
⅛ teaspoon ground ginger
50 g (¼ cup) soft brown sugar
70 g (⅓ cup) pitted dates, chopped
150 g (1½ cups) walnuts, chopped
1 egg
1 large Granny Smith apple
2½ tablespoons caster sugar
60 g (½ cup) plain flour

Preheat the oven to 170°C (325°F/ Gas 3). Lightly grease a 20 x 30 cm baking tin and line with baking paper, hanging over on the two long sides.

Melt 20 g of the butter and the golden syrup in a saucepan. Remove from the heat and stir in the cider. Sift the flour and ginger into a bowl. Stir in the brown sugar, dates and half the nuts. Beat in the golden syrup mixture and egg until smooth. Spoon into the tin.

Peel, core and thinly slice the apple, then cut into 1.5 cm pieces. Melt the remaining butter in a small saucepan, add the caster sugar, flour, apple and remaining nuts and stir well. Spread over the cake mixture. Bake for 30 minutes, or until golden and a skewer comes out clean. Cool in the tin, remove and cut into squares.

Makes 24 pieces

Pineapple upside-down cake

20 g unsalted butter, melted
2 tablespoons firmly packed soft
 brown sugar
440 g tin pineapple rings in natural
 juice
90 g unsalted butter, extra, softened
125 g (½ cup) caster sugar
2 eggs, lightly beaten
1 teaspoon vanilla essence
125 g (1 cup) self-raising flour

Preheat the oven to 180°C (350°F/ Gas 4). Grease a 20 cm ring tin. Pour the melted butter into the base of the tin and tip to evenly coat. Sprinkle with the brown sugar. Drain the pineapple and reserve 80 ml (⅓ cup) of the juice. Cut the pineapple rings in half and arrange on the base.

Beat the extra butter and the caster sugar with electric beaters until light and creamy. Gradually add the egg, beating well after each addition. Add the vanilla essence and beat until combined. Fold in the flour alternately with the reserved juice, using a metal spoon.

Spoon the mixture evenly over the pineapple and smooth the surface. Bake for 35–40 minutes, or until a skewer comes out clean when inserted into the centre of the cake. Leave in the tin for 10 minutes before turning out onto a wire rack to cool.

Serves 6–8

Orange-scented date crescents

185 g (1 cup) pitted dates, chopped
3 teaspoons finely grated orange zest
2 teaspoons orange flower water or
    orange juice
125 g unsalted butter, cubed and
    softened
125 g (½ cup) caster sugar
1 egg
250 g (2 cups) plain flour, sifted
1 teaspoon baking powder
sugar, to sprinkle

Put the dates and 1 tablespoon water in a small pan. Stir over low heat for 2–3 minutes, or until the dates are soft. Remove from the heat and stir in 1 teaspoon of the zest and 1 teaspoon of the orange flower water. Cool.

Line two baking trays with baking paper. Beat the butter, caster sugar, the remaining orange zest and orange flower water until creamy. Add the egg and beat until well combined.

Mix in the combined flour and baking powder until a smooth dough forms. Cover with plastic wrap and refrigerate for 30 minutes. Put half the dough between two sheets of baking paper and roll out to 5 mm thick. Refrigerate again if the dough is too soft. Preheat the oven to 180°C (350°F/Gas 4).

Cut out ten 6.5 cm circles from the dough with a fluted cutter. Put 1 small teaspoon of filling onto each circle and fold over to form a crescent, gently pressing the edges to seal. The pastry should be well filled with the mixture. Repeat with the remaining dough.

Lay on the trays, brush the tops with water and sprinkle with the sugar. Bake for 10–15 minutes, or until lightly golden. Cool on a wire rack.

Makes about 25

Saffron spice cake

250 ml (1 cup) freshly squeezed
  orange juice
1 tablespoon finely grated orange zest
¼ teaspoon saffron threads
3 eggs
155 g (1¼ cups) icing sugar
250 g (2 cups) self-raising flour
370 g (3⅔ cups) ground almonds
125 g unsalted butter, melted
icing sugar, extra, to dust
thick (double) cream, to serve

Preheat the oven to 180°C (350°F/
Gas 4). Lightly grease a 22 cm round
cake tin and line the base with baking
paper. Combine the orange juice, zest
and saffron in a small saucepan and
bring to the boil. Lower the heat and
simmer for 1 minute. Leave to cool.

Beat the eggs and icing sugar with
electric beaters until light and creamy.
Fold in the sifted flour, almonds,
orange juice mixture and butter with a
metal spoon until just combined and
the mixture is just smooth. Spoon the
mixture into the prepared tin.

Bake for 1 hour, or until a skewer
comes out clean when inserted into
the centre of the cake. Leave in the
tin for 15 minutes before turning onto
a wire rack to cool. Dust with a little
icing sugar and serve with cream.

Serves 8

Lemon squares

125 g unsalted butter
75 g (¹⁄₃ cup) caster sugar
155 g (1¹⁄₄ cups) plain flour, sifted
icing sugar, to dust

Topping
4 eggs, lightly beaten
250 g (1 cup) caster sugar
60 ml (¹⁄₄ cup) lemon juice
1 teaspoon finely grated lemon zest
30 g (¹⁄₄ cup) plain flour
¹⁄₂ teaspoon baking powder

Preheat the oven to 180°C (350°F/ Gas 4). Lightly grease a 20 x 30 cm baking tin and line with baking paper, leaving the paper hanging over two opposite sides.

Cream the butter and sugar with electric beaters until pale and fluffy. Fold in the flour with a metal spoon. Press into the tin and bake for 20 minutes, or until golden and firm. Leave to cool.

Beat the eggs and sugar with electric beaters for 2 minutes, or until light and fluffy. Stir in the lemon juice and lemon zest. Sift together the flour and baking powder and gradually whisk into the egg mixture. Pour onto the base. Bake for 25 minutes, or until just firm. Cool in the tin and dust with icing sugar.

Makes 30 pieces

Almond, orange and cardamom biscotti

2 eggs
155 g (²/₃ cup) firmly packed soft
  brown sugar
125 g (1 cup) self-raising flour
90 g (³/₄ cup) plain flour
125 g (1¹/₄ cups) almonds
1 tablespoon finely grated orange zest
¹/₄ teaspoon ground cardamom

Preheat the oven to 160°C (315°F/ Gas 2–3). Line a baking tray with baking paper.

Beat the eggs and sugar in a bowl with electric beaters until pale and creamy. Sift the self-raising and plain flours into the bowl, then add the almonds, orange zest and cardamom and mix to a soft dough.

Turn out the dough onto a lightly floured work surface. Divide the mixture into two portions, shaping it into two 5 x 20 cm loaves.

Bake for 35–40 minutes, or until lightly golden. Transfer to a wire rack to cool. Cut the loaves into 1 cm diagonal slices with a large serrated bread knife. The biscotti will be crumbly on the edges so work slowly and, if possible, try to hold the sides as you cut.

Arrange the slices on baking trays in a single layer. Return to the oven for 10 minutes on each side. Don't worry if they don't seem fully dry as they will become crisp on cooling. Allow the biscotti to cool before serving.

Makes 40

Storage: Biscotti will store in an airtight container for 2–3 weeks.

Golden ginger pear cake

175 g (½ cup) golden syrup
250 g (2 cups) self-raising flour
2½ teaspoons ground ginger
165 g (¾ cup) firmly packed soft
  brown sugar
2 pears (about 200 g), peeled, halved
  and thinly sliced
3 eggs, lightly beaten
125 ml (½ cup) buttermilk
150 g unsalted butter, chopped

Preheat the oven to 180°C (350°F/ Gas 4). Grease a deep 18 cm round cake tin and line the base with baking paper. Pour half of the golden syrup over the base of the tin, spreading evenly with a metal spoon, which has been run under hot water.

Sift the flour and ground ginger into a bowl. Add the sugar and pear, then the egg, buttermilk and 125 g of the butter, melted, and stir until just combined and smooth.

Spoon the mixture into the prepared tin and bake for 1 hour 30 minutes, or until a skewer comes out clean when inserted into the centre of the cake. Leave in the tin for 10 minutes, then carefully invert onto a serving plate.

Heat the remaining golden syrup and the remaining butter in a saucepan over low heat until the butter has melted. Spoon the sauce evenly over the cake and serve warm. If desired, serve with ice cream or cream.

Serves 8

Chocolate and glacé cherry slice

125 g (1 cup) plain flour
40 g (1/3 cup) cocoa powder
90 g (1/3 cup) caster sugar
125 g unsalted butter, melted
1 teaspoon vanilla essence
420 g (2 cups) glacé cherries, finely
   chopped
60 g (1/2 cup) icing sugar
135 g (1 1/2 cups) desiccated coconut
160 g (1/2 cup) condensed milk
60 g unsalted butter, melted
50 g copha (white vegetable
   shortening), melted
150 g dark cooking chocolate
25 g unsalted butter, extra

Preheat the oven to 180°C (350°F/ Gas 4). Lightly grease an 18 x 27 cm shallow baking tin and line with baking paper, leaving the paper hanging over the two long sides.

Sift the flour, cocoa and sugar into a bowl, add the butter and vanilla, and mix to form a dough. Gather together and turn onto a well-floured surface. Press together for 1 minute, then press into the base of the tin. Chill for 20 minutes. Cover with baking paper and baking beads or uncooked rice and bake for 10–15 minutes. Remove the paper and beads and bake for 5 minutes. Cool.

Combine the cherries, icing sugar and coconut. Stir in the condensed milk, butter and copha, then spread over the base. Chill for 30 minutes.

Chop the chocolate and extra butter into small even-sized pieces and place in a heatproof bowl. Bring a saucepan of water to the boil and remove from the heat. Sit the bowl over the pan, making sure the bowl doesn't touch the water. Allow to stand, stirring occasionally until melted. Pour over the cooled cherry mixture, then chill until set.

Makes 28 pieces

Honey, banana and macadamia cake

125 g unsalted butter, chopped
440 g (1¼ cups) honey
310 g (2½ cups) self-raising flour
1½ teaspoons mixed spice
3 or 4 large carrots (220 g), coarsely
  grated
1 large ripe banana, mashed
120 g (¾ cup) macadamia nuts,
  chopped
3 eggs, lightly beaten

Ricotta honey icing
375 g (1½ cups) smooth ricotta
  cheese
70 g unsalted butter, softened
2 tablespoons honey

Preheat the oven to 180°C (350°F/ Gas 4). Grease a 26 cm round cake tin and line the base with baking paper. Melt the butter and honey in a saucepan, stirring until combined. Leave to cool.

Sift the flour and mixed spice into a large bowl. Add the carrot, banana, macadamias, egg and honey mixture, stirring until the mixture is just combined and smooth.

Spoon the mixture into the prepared tin and bake for 1 hour 10 minutes, or until a skewer comes out clean when inserted into the centre of the cake. Leave in the tin for 15 minutes before carefully turning out onto a wire rack to cool.

To make the ricotta honey icing, beat the ricotta, butter and honey with electric beaters for 2–3 minutes, or until light and creamy. Spread the icing over the top the cake.

Serves 8–10

Chocolate peanut squares

200 g dark chocolate
125 g unsalted butter
230 g (1 cup) firmly packed soft
  brown sugar
65 g (¼ cup) crunchy peanut butter
2 eggs
125 g (1 cup) plain flour
30 g (¼ cup) self-raising flour
80 g (½ cup) unsalted roasted
  peanuts, roughly chopped
100 g dark chocolate, extra, broken
  into pieces

Preheat the oven to 170°C (325°F/ Gas 3). Lightly grease an 18 x 27 cm baking tin and line with baking paper, hanging over the two long sides.

Chop the chocolate into small even-sized pieces and place in a heatproof bowl. Bring a saucepan of water to the boil and remove from the heat. Sit the bowl over the pan — ensure the bowl doesn't touch the water. Allow to stand, stirring occasionally until melted. Allow to cool.

Cream the butter, sugar and peanut butter with electric beaters until thick. Add the eggs one at a time, beating well after each addition. Stir in the chocolate, sifted flours and peanuts.

Spread the mixture into the tin and gently press the pieces of dark chocolate evenly into the surface. Bake for 30 minutes, or until a skewer inserted into the centre comes out clean. Cool in the tin.

Makes 24 pieces

Rhubarb yoghurt cake

150 g (1¼ cups) finely sliced fresh
rhubarb
310 g (2½ cups) self-raising flour,
sifted
250 g (1 cup) caster sugar
1 teaspoon vanilla essence
2 eggs, lightly beaten
125 g (½ cup) plain yoghurt
1 tablespoon rosewater
125 g unsalted butter, melted

Preheat the oven to 180°C (350°F/
Gas 4). Lightly grease a 23 cm round
cake tin and line the base with baking
paper. Combine the rhubarb, flour
and sugar in a bowl.

Add the vanilla essence, egg, yoghurt,
rosewater and melted butter, stirring
until the mixture is just combined.

Spoon the mixture into the cake tin
and bake for 1 hour, or until a skewer
comes out clean when inserted into
the centre of the cake. Leave in the
tin for 15 minutes before turning out
onto a wire rack. Serve with yoghurt
or cream, if desired.

Serves 8

Almond shortbreads

250 g unsalted butter
250 g (2 cups) plain flour
1 teaspoon baking powder
90 g (3/4 cup) icing sugar, sifted
1 egg yolk
1 teaspoon vanilla essence
1 tablespoon ouzo
100 g (3/4 cup) slivered almonds,
   ground to a medium-fine texture
4 tablespoons ground almonds
60 g (1/2 cup) icing sugar, extra,
   to dust

Melt the butter over low heat in a small heavy-based saucepan, without stirring or shaking the pan. Carefully pour the clear butter into another container, leaving the white sediment in the pan to be discarded. Refrigerate for 1 hour. Preheat the oven to 170°C (325°F/Gas 3) and line two baking trays with baking paper.

In a bowl, sift the flour and baking powder together. Using electric beaters, beat the chilled butter until light and fluffy. Gradually add the icing sugar and combine well. Add the egg yolk, vanilla and ouzo and beat until just combined. Fold in the flour, the ground slivered almonds and the ground almonds.

Shape heaped tablespoons of mixture into crescents, place on the baking trays and bake for 12 minutes, or until lightly coloured. Remove from the oven and dust liberally with icing sugar. Allow to cool a little on the trays.

Line a baking tray with baking paper and dust the paper with icing sugar. Lift the warm biscuits onto this and dust again with icing sugar. When the biscuits are cool, dust them once again with icing sugar before storing them in an airtight container.

Makes 22

Sour cherry cake

125 g unsalted butter, softened
185 g ($^3/_4$ cup) caster sugar
2 eggs, lightly beaten
95 g (1 cup) ground almonds
125 g (1 cup) self-raising flour
60 g ($^1/_2$ cup) plain flour
125 ml ($^1/_2$ cup) milk
680 g jar pitted morello cherries,
  well drained

Preheat the oven to 180°C (350°F/ Gas 4). Grease and flour a 23 cm fluted baba tin, shaking out the excess flour.

Beat the butter and sugar with electric beaters until pale but not creamy. Add the egg gradually, beating well after each addition.

Stir in the ground almonds, then fold in the sifted flours alternately with the milk. Gently fold in the cherries. Spoon the mixture into the prepared tin and smooth the surface.

Bake for 50 minutes, or until a skewer comes out clean when inserted into the centre of the cake. Leave to cool in the tin for 10 minutes before turning out onto a wire rack to cool. If desired, dust with icing sugar before serving.

Serves 8–10

Note: This cake is best eaten on the day it is made.

Italian orange biscuits

175 g (1½ cups) plain flour
200 g (1⅔ cups) semolina or fine
  polenta
100 g (½ cup) caster sugar
100 g unsalted butter, softened
2½ teaspoons grated orange zest
2 eggs

Put the flour, semolina, sugar, butter, orange zest, eggs and a pinch of salt in a food processor and mix until smooth. Chill the mixture in the fridge for 15 minutes.

Preheat the oven to 190°C (375°F/ Gas 5). Grease a baking tray and place a teaspoon of the mixture on the tray. Lightly moisten your fingers with a little water and press the mixture down to flatten it. Don't use too much water or it will affect the texture of the biscuits. Leave space between the biscuits as the biscuits will expand during cooking.

Bake for about 15 minutes, or until the edge of the biscuit is dark golden brown. Remove from the oven, scoop off the tray with a metal spatula and cool on a wire rack. If you are baking the biscuits in batches, make sure the tray is greased each time you use it.

Makes 45

Orange and lemon syrup cake

3 lemons
3 oranges
250 g unsalted butter, chilled and
  chopped
685 g (2¾ cups) caster sugar
6 eggs, lightly beaten
375 ml (1½ cups) milk
375 g (3 cups) self-raising flour, sifted

Preheat the oven to 160°C (315°F/ Gas 2–3). Grease a 24 cm springform tin and line the base and side with baking paper. Finely grate the zest from the lemons and oranges to give 3 tablespoons of each, then squeeze the fruit to give 185 ml (¾ cup) juice from each. Heat the butter, 500 g (2 cups) of the sugar and 1 tablespoon each of the lemon and orange zest in a saucepan over low heat, stirring until melted. Pour into a bowl.

Add half the egg, 185 ml (¾ cup) of the milk and 185 g (1½ cups) of the flour to the bowl, beating with electric beaters until just combined. Add the remaining egg, milk and flour and beat until smooth — do not overmix. Pour into the tin and bake for 1 hour 15 minutes, or until a skewer comes out clean when inserted into the centre of the cake — cover with foil if it browns too much. Cool in the tin.

Combine the fruit juices, the remaining zests and sugar and 125 ml (½ cup) water in a pan and stir over low heat until the sugar has dissolved. Increase the heat and bring to the boil for 10 minutes, or until it thickens and reduces slightly. Pour the hot syrup over the cool cake. Cool in the tin for 10 minutes, then remove.

Serves 10–12

Rum and raisin slice

60 g (½ cup) raisins
80 ml (⅓ cup) dark rum
200 g dark chocolate
60 g unsalted butter
125 g (½ cup) caster sugar
250 ml (1 cup) thick (double) cream
125 g (1 cup) plain flour
3 eggs, lightly beaten
cocoa powder, to dust

Preheat the oven to 180°C (350°F/ Gas 4). Lightly grease an 18 x 28 cm shallow baking tin and line with baking paper, hanging over on two opposite sides.

Combine the raisins and rum. Chop the chocolate and butter into small even-sized pieces and place in a heatproof bowl. Bring a saucepan of water to the boil and remove from the heat. Sit the bowl over the pan — ensure the bowl doesn't touch the water. Allow to stand, stirring occasionally until melted. Stir in the caster sugar and cream.

Sift the flour into a bowl. Add the raisins, chocolate mixture and eggs and mix well. Pour into the tin and smooth the surface. Bake for 25–30 minutes, or until just set. Cool completely, then refrigerate overnight before cutting into small pieces. Sprinkle liberally with cocoa powder.

Makes 20 pieces

Blueberry muffins

375 g (3 cups) plain flour
1 tablespoon baking powder
165 g (³⁄₄ cup) firmly packed soft
  brown sugar
125 g unsalted butter, melted
2 eggs, lightly beaten
250 ml (1 cup) milk
185 g (1¹⁄₄ cups) fresh or thawed
  frozen blueberries

Preheat the oven to 210°C (415°F/ Gas 6–7). Grease or brush two trays of six 125 ml (¹⁄₂ cup) muffin holes with melted butter or oil. Sift the flour and baking powder into a large bowl. Stir in the sugar and make a well in the centre.

Add the combined melted butter, eggs and milk all at once, and fold until just combined. Do not overmix — the batter should look quite lumpy.

Fold in the blueberries. Spoon the batter into the prepared tin. Bake for 20 minutes, or until golden brown. Cool on a wire rack.

Makes 12

Pear upside-down cake

2 tablespoons soft brown sugar
425 g tin pear halves in syrup
250 g (2 cups) self-raising flour
125 g unsalted butter
185 g (³/₄ cup) caster sugar
2 eggs, lightly beaten

Preheat the oven to 180°C (350°F/ Gas 4). Grease a 21 x 14 x 7 cm loaf tin and line the base with baking paper. Sprinkle the brown sugar evenly over the base of the tin. Drain the pears and reserve the syrup. Cut the pears in half and arrange, cut-side-down, over the base.

Sift the flour into a large bowl and make a well in the centre. Melt the butter and caster sugar in a small saucepan over low heat, stirring until the sugar has dissolved. Remove from the heat. Combine the egg with the reserved syrup. Add both the butter and the egg mixtures to the flour and stir with a wooden spoon until combined — do not overbeat. Spoon the mixture over the pears and smooth the surface.

Bake for 50 minutes, or until a skewer comes out clean when inserted into the centre of the cake. Leave in the tin for 15 minutes (this standing time allows the pears to better adhere to the cake) before turning out onto a wire rack to cool.

Serves 6–8

Peanut toffee shortbread

290 g unsalted butter
125 g (½ cup) caster sugar
1 egg
185 g (1½ cups) plain flour, sifted
60 g (½ cup) self-raising flour, sifted
180 g (1 cup) soft brown sugar
2 tablespoons golden syrup
½ teaspoon lemon juice
400 g (2½ cups) roasted unsalted
  peanuts

Preheat the oven to 180°C (350°F/ Gas 4). Lightly grease an 18 x 27 cm baking tin and line the base and sides with baking paper hanging over the two long sides.

Cream 110 g of butter and the caster sugar with electric beaters until light and fluffy. Add the egg and beat well. Fold in the sifted flours with a large metal spoon until just combined. Press into the tin and bake for 15 minutes, or until firm and lightly coloured. Cool for 10 minutes.

Place the brown sugar, golden syrup, lemon juice and remaining butter in a saucepan. Stir over low heat until the sugar has dissolved. Simmer, stirring, for 5 minutes. Stir in the peanuts. Spread evenly over the base using two spoons — be careful as the mixture is very hot. Bake for a further 5 minutes. Leave to cool in the tin for 15 minutes, then turn out and cut into fingers.

Makes 18 pieces

Blueberry shortcake

100 g (³/₄ cup) hazelnuts
280 g (2¹/₄ cups) self-raising flour
1¹/₂ teaspoons ground cinnamon
165 g (³/₄ cup) demerara sugar
150 g unsalted butter, chopped
2 eggs
160 g (¹/₂ cup) blueberry jam
1 tablespoon demerara sugar, extra

Preheat the oven to 180°C (350°F/ Gas 4). Grease a deep 20 cm round cake tin and line the base with baking paper. Spread the hazelnuts on a baking tray and bake them for 5–10 minutes, or until lightly golden. Place in a clean tea towel and rub together to remove the skins, then roughly chop.

Mix the flour, cinnamon, sugar, butter and half the hazelnuts in a food processor in short bursts until finely chopped. Add the eggs and process until well combined. Press half the mixture onto the base of the tin, then spread the jam evenly over the mixture. Lightly knead the remaining hazelnuts into the remaining dough, then press evenly over the jam layer.

Sprinkle the extra sugar over the top and bake for 50 minutes, or until a skewer comes out clean when inserted into the centre of the cake. Leave in the tin for 15 minutes before carefully turning out onto a wire rack to cool. If desired, garnish with fresh blueberries and serve with thick cream.

Serves 8–10

Peppermint and chocolate slice

220 g (1¾ cups) plain flour
1 teaspoon baking powder
95 g (½ cup) soft brown sugar
180 g unsalted butter, melted
60 g copha (white vegetable shortening)
435 g (3½ cups) icing sugar, sifted
1 teaspoon peppermint essence
2 tablespoons milk
2 tablespoons cream
300 g dark cooking chocolate
70 g unsalted butter, extra

Preheat the oven to 180°C (350°F/ Gas 4). Grease a 20 x 30 cm baking tin and line with baking paper, leaving the paper hanging over the two long sides of the tin.

Sift together the flour and baking powder and add the brown sugar. Stir in the melted butter, press into the tin and bake for 20 minutes. Cool.

Melt the copha in a saucepan over medium heat. Stir in the icing sugar, peppermint essence, milk and cream. Mix well and pour over the pastry base. Leave to set.

Chop the chocolate and extra butter into small even-sized pieces and place in a heatproof bowl. Bring a saucepan of water to the boil and remove from the heat. Sit the bowl over the pan, making sure the bowl doesn't touch the water. Stand, stirring occasionally, until melted and combined. Cool slightly, then spread over the icing. Chill until set, then cut into pieces.

Makes 20 pieces

Chocolate and almond torte

150 g (1²/₃ cups) flaked or whole
  (1 cup) almonds
1 slice pandoro sweet cake or 1 small
  brioche (about 40 g)
300 g dark chocolate
2 tablespoons brandy
150 g unsalted butter, softened
150 g (²/₃ cup) caster sugar
4 eggs
1 teaspoon vanilla extract (optional)
200 g (1 cup) mascarpone
cocoa powder, to dust
crème fraîche, to serve

Preheat the oven to 170°C (325°F/ Gas 3). Toast the almonds in the oven for 8–10 minutes until golden brown, keeping a close eye on them.

Put the almonds and pandoro in a food processor and process until the mixture resembles coarse breadcrumbs. Grease a 23 cm springform tin with butter. Tip some of the mixture into the tin and shake it around to coat the bottom and side. Put the remaining nut mixture aside.

Gently melt the chocolate and brandy in a heatproof bowl set over a saucepan of simmering water, making sure the bowl does not touch the water. Stir occasionally until the chocolate has melted — do not overstir or the cocoa butter in the chocolate can separate. Cool slightly.

Cream the butter and sugar in the food processor until light and pale. Add the chocolate, eggs, vanilla and mascarpone. Add the remaining nut mixture and mix well. Tip into the tin.

Bake for 50–60 minutes or until just set. Rest in the tin for 15 minutes before taking out. Dust with a little cocoa when cool and serve with crème fraîche.

Serves 8

Banana and honey loaf

125 g unsalted butter, softened
140 g ($^3/_4$ cup) soft brown sugar
2 eggs, lightly beaten
2 tablespoons honey
1 large (175 g) ripe banana, cut into
  chunks
225 g (1$^1/_2$ cups) wholemeal
  self-raising flour
2 teaspoons ground cinnamon

Preheat the oven to 180°C (350°F/
Gas 4). Grease a 22 x 12 cm loaf tin.
Combine the butter and sugar in a
food processor for 1 minute, or until
lighter in colour. Add the egg and
process until combined.

Put 1 tablespoon of the honey in a
saucepan over low heat and warm for
1 minute, or until runny. Add to the
food processor with the banana
and blend until smooth. Add the
flour and cinnamon and process until
well combined.

Spoon evenly into the loaf tin and
bake for 35–40 minutes, or until a
skewer comes out clean when
inserted into the centre of the cake.
Leave in the tin for 5 minutes before
turning out onto a wire rack. Warm
the remaining honey in a saucepan
over low heat for 1 minute, or until
runny. Brush the warm cake with the
warm honey. Serve warm or cool.

Serves 8

Note: Alternatively, warm the honey in
the microwave on Medium High (70%)
for 30 seconds.
Variation: Fold 60 g ($^1/_2$ cup) chopped
walnuts or pecans through the
mixture before spooning the mixture
into the loaf tin.

Dried fruit and chocolate pillows

Cream cheese pastry
90 g (⅓ cup) cream cheese, softened
60 g (¼ cup) caster sugar
1 egg yolk
3 tablespoons milk
185 g (1½ cups) plain flour
1 teaspoon baking powder
1 egg white, to glaze

Dried fruit filling
60 g (⅓ cup) chopped dried figs
95 g (½ cup) chopped dried apricots
60 g (½ cup) raisins, chopped
60 g dark chocolate, chopped
½ teaspoon grated lemon zest
80 g (¼ cup) clear honey
large pinch ground allspice
large pinch ground cinnamon

To make the cream cheese pastry, beat the cheese and sugar until fluffy. Beat in the egg yolk and milk, then sift in the flour, a pinch of salt and the baking powder and form into a smooth dough. Cover with plastic wrap and refrigerate for 2 hours.

To make the dried fruit filling, put all the ingredients in a food processor and process in short bursts until finely chopped.

Preheat the oven to 180°C (350°F/ Gas 4). Divide the fruit filling into three portions and roll into 32 cm long ropes. Divide the pastry into three and, on a lightly floured surface, roll out to 10 x 32 cm rectangles.

Brush one length of a rectangle with water. Lay a portion of filling on the strip of pastry near the dry side. Roll the pastry over and press to seal, then cut into eight diagonal pieces and lay, seam-side-down, on an ungreased baking tray. Repeat with the remaining pastry and filling.

Mix the egg white with 1 tablespoon of cold water and glaze the biscuits, then bake for 13–15 minutes, or until golden. Leave for 2–3 minutes, then cool on a wire rack.

Makes 24

Pistachio, yoghurt and cardamom cake

150 g (1 cup) unsalted pistachio nuts
1/2 teaspoon ground cardamom
150 g unsalted butter, chopped
185 g (1 1/2 cups) self-raising flour
310 g (1 1/4 cups) caster sugar
3 eggs
125 g (1/2 cup) plain yoghurt
1 lime

Preheat the oven to 180°C (350°F/ Gas 4). Grease a 20 cm round cake tin and line the base with baking paper. Place the pistachios and cardamom in a food processor and pulse until just chopped. Add the butter, flour and 185 g (3/4 cup) of the caster sugar and pulse for 20 seconds, or until crumbly. Add the combined eggs and yoghurt and pulse for 10 seconds, or until just combined. Spoon into the tin and smooth the surface.

Bake for 45–50 minutes, or until a skewer comes out clean when inserted into the centre of the cake.

To make the syrup, peel the zest off the lime with a vegetable peeler — remove any white pith from the zest. Place the remaining caster sugar and 100 ml water in a saucepan and stir over low heat until the sugar has dissolved. Bring to the boil, then add the lime zest and cook for 5 minutes. Strain and cool slightly. Pierce the cake with a few skewer holes and pour the hot syrup over the cooled cake.

Serves 8

Ginger panforte slice

40 g (1/3 cup) plain flour
1 tablespoon cocoa powder
1 teaspoon ground ginger
1/2 teaspoon ground cardamom
1 teaspoon ground cinnamon
125 g (3/4 cup) dried figs, chopped
50 g (1/4 cup) glacé ginger, chopped
50 g (1/4 cup) glacé pineapple,
  chopped
50 g (1/4 cup) glacé apricots, chopped
50 g (1/4 cup) chopped mixed peel
175 g (1 cup) blanched almonds,
  toasted (see page 390)
90 g (1/3 cup) caster sugar
90 g (1/4 cup) honey

Preheat the oven to 160°C (315°F/ Gas 2–3). Lightly grease a 7 x 25 cm shallow baking tin and line with baking paper, hanging over at the two short ends.

Sift the flour, cocoa, ginger and spices into a large bowl. Add the fruit and almonds.

Heat the caster sugar, honey and 2 teaspoons water in a small saucepan over low heat, stirring until melted and it just comes to the boil. Pour onto the dry ingredients and mix well. Press the mixture into the tin and bake for 35–40 minutes, or until just firm. Cool in the tin, then chill until firm. Cut into thin slices.

Makes 20 pieces

Honey picnic cake

300 g (1 ¼ cups) sour cream
165 g (¾ cup) firmly packed soft
   brown sugar
1 egg
300 g (2 cups) wholemeal plain flour
1 teaspoon baking powder
3 tablespoons honey, warmed
50 g (½ cup) pecan nuts, chopped

Preheat the oven to 150°C (300°F/ Gas 2). Grease a 22 x 12 cm loaf tin and line the base and the two long sides with baking paper.

Blend the sour cream, sugar and egg in a food processor until combined. Add the flour and baking powder and process until well blended. Add the honey and process until mixed. Add the nuts and process just long enough for them to mix through.

Spoon into the prepared tin and bake for 1 hour, or until a skewer comes out clean when inserted into the centre of the cake. Leave in the tin for 15 minutes before turning out onto a wire rack to cool.

Serves 8–10

Note: This cake is delicious served plain or buttered.

Lemon ricotta slice

220 g (1³/4 cups) plain flour
1 teaspoon baking powder
180 g unsalted butter, melted
210 g (1 cup) caster sugar
4 eggs
350 g (1¹/3 cups) ricotta cheese
200 ml (³/4 cup) cream
2 tablespoons lemon zest
185 ml (³/4 cup) lemon juice
icing sugar, to dust

Preheat the oven to 180°C (350°F/ Gas 4). Lightly grease a 20 x 30 cm baking tin and line with baking paper, hanging over the two long sides.

Put the flour, baking powder, butter and half of the caster sugar in a food processor and process in short bursts until the mixture comes together in a ball. Add 1 egg and process until combined.

Press the mixture into the tin. Bake for 15 minutes. Remove from the oven. Reduce the oven to 150°C (300°F/Gas 2).

Place the ricotta, cream, lemon zest and juice, the remaining sugar and remaining eggs in the cleaned food processor and combine the ingredients for 1–2 seconds. Pour onto the pastry base and bake for 25–30 minutes — the slice will still have a slight wobble at this stage. Cool slightly, then refrigerate for 2 hours to firm. Cut into pieces. Dust with icing sugar and serve.

Makes 15 pieces

Individual milk chocolate cakes

75 g unsalted butter
75 g milk chocolate, chopped
80 g (⅓ cup) firmly packed brown
   sugar
2 eggs, lightly beaten
60 g (½ cup) self-raising flour, sifted

Ganache
80 g milk chocolate, chopped
2 tablespoons thick (double) cream

Preheat the oven to 160°C (315°F/ Gas 2–3). Line a flat-bottomed 12-hole cupcake tray with paper patty cases. Put the butter and chocolate in a heatproof bowl and place over a saucepan of simmering water — make sure the base of the bowl doesn't touch the water. Stir until melted and combined. Remove the bowl from the heat, add the sugar and egg and mix. Stir in the flour.

Transfer the mixture to a measuring jug and pour into the patty cases. Bake for 20–25 minutes, or until cooked. Leave in the tin for 10 minutes, then transfer to a wire rack to cool.

To make the ganache, place the chocolate and cream in a heatproof bowl. Place over a saucepan of simmering water — ensure the base of the bowl doesn't touch the water. Once the chocolate has almost melted, remove the bowl from the heat and stir until the remaining chocolate has melted and the mixture is smooth. Allow to cool for about 8 minutes, or until thickened slightly. Return the cakes to the cold patty tin, to keep them stable while you spread one heaped teaspoon of ganache over the top. If desired, decorate with gold cachous.

Makes 12

Scottish shortbread

250 g unsalted butter, softened
160 g (²/₃ cup) caster sugar
210 g (1²/₃ cups) plain flour
90 g (½ cup) rice flour
1 teaspoon sugar

Preheat the oven to 160°C (315°F/ Gas 2–3). Brush a 28 cm round pizza tray with melted butter or oil and line with baking paper.

Beat the butter and sugar with electric beaters in a small bowl until light and creamy. Transfer to a large bowl and add the sifted flours. Mix to a soft dough with a flat-bladed knife. Lift the dough onto a lightly floured work surface and knead for 30 seconds, or until smooth.

Transfer to the pizza tray and press into a 25 cm round (the tray must be larger than the uncooked shortbread as the mixture will spread during cooking). Pinch and flute around the edge with your fingers to decorate. Prick the surface lightly with a fork and mark into 16 segments with a sharp knife. Sprinkle with sugar and bake on the middle shelf of the oven for 35 minutes, or until firm and lightly golden. Allow the shortbread to cool on the tray.

Makes 16 pieces

Spiced Christmas muffins

325 g (1¾ cups) mixed dried fruit
80 ml (⅓ cup) rum or brandy
310 g (2½ cups) self-raising flour
1 teaspoon mixed spice
1 teaspoon ground cinnamon
½ teaspoon ground nutmeg
155 g (⅔ cup) firmly packed soft
  brown sugar
125 ml (½ cup) milk
1 egg, lightly beaten
2 tablespoons apricot jam
½ teaspoon very finely grated
  lemon zest
½ teaspoon very finely grated
  orange zest
125 g unsalted butter, melted
  and cooled
125 g soft ready-made icing
icing sugar, to dust
2 tablespoons apricot jam, extra,
  warmed and sieved
red and green glacé cherries, for
  decoration

Place the dried fruit and rum in a large bowl and mix together. Cover and marinate, stirring often, for 1–2 hours.

Preheat the oven to 200°C (400°F/ Gas 6). Line 12 muffin holes with muffin papers. Sift the flour, mixed spice, cinnamon and nutmeg into a large bowl and stir in the brown sugar. Make a well in the centre.

Put the milk, egg, apricot jam, lemon and orange zest and melted butter in a jug, mix together and pour into the well. Stir in the dried fruit mixture. Fold gently until just combined — the batter should be lumpy.

Divide the mixture evenly among the muffin holes. Bake for 20 minutes, or until a skewer inserted in the middle of the muffins comes out clean. Cool in the tins for 5 minutes, then transfer to a wire rack to cool completely.

Place the ready-made icing on a work surface dusted with a little icing sugar. Roll out to 2 mm thick and, using a 7 cm fluted round cutter, cut out 12 rounds. Brush the muffin tops with the extra apricot jam and top each with a round of icing. Decorate with whole or halved red glacé cherries and small 'leaves' of green glacé cherries.

Makes 12 muffins

Butter almond torte

120 g unsalted butter, chopped
90 ml milk
2 eggs
1 teaspoon vanilla essence
250 g (2 cups) caster sugar
135 g (1 cup) plain flour
2 teaspoons baking powder
100 g ($^3/_4$ cup) slivered almonds

Preheat the oven to 180°C (350°F/ Gas 4). Line the base of a 22 cm springform tin with foil and lightly grease the base and side. Heat 60 g of the butter and 80 ml of the milk in a small saucepan until the butter has melted.

Beat the eggs, vanilla and 185 g ($^3/_4$ cup) of the sugar with electric beaters until thick and creamy. Stir in the butter and milk mixture. Sift in 125 g of the flour and the baking powder and stir to combine — the mixture will be thin. Pour into the tin and bake for 50 minutes.

Melt the remaining butter in a small saucepan. Stir in the almonds with the remaining sugar, flour and milk and stir until combined. Quickly spoon the topping onto the cake (the centre will still be uncooked) starting from the outside edges and avoid piling the topping in the centre. Return to the oven for a further 10–15 minutes, or until golden and cooked through. Cool in the tin before inverting onto a wire rack.

Serves 8–10

Note: This torte is great served as a dessert with whipped cream.

Polenta cake

45 g (⅓ cup) sultanas
2 tablespoons brandy
225 g (1 cup) ricotta cheese
250 g (1 cup) caster sugar
225 g (1½ cups) polenta
pinch of grated nutmeg
½ teaspoon grated lemon zest
¼ teaspoon vanilla extract
20 g unsalted butter, chilled and cut
  into small cubes
2 tablespoons pine nuts
icing sugar, to dust
whipped cream, to serve

Put the sultanas and brandy in a small bowl with enough water to cover them and leave for 30 minutes. Drain and dry well on paper towels.

Preheat the oven to 160°C (315°F/ Gas 2–3) and grease a 25 cm loose-bottomed or springform cake tin with a tight-fitting base.

Put the ricotta in a large bowl and add 450 ml cold water. Beat with a wire whisk or electric beaters until smooth. Don't be alarmed by the thinness of the mixture — it can be very liquid, depending on the brand of ricotta used. Add the sugar and beat until smooth, then stir in the polenta, nutmeg, lemon zest, vanilla extract and sultanas.

Pour the mixture into the tin. Dot the surface with butter and sprinkle the pine nuts on top. Put the tin on a baking tray to catch any drips and bake for about 1 hour 30 minutes, or until golden and set. Serve warm or cold, dusted with icing sugar and accompanied with whipped cream.

Serves 8–10

Coffee cupcakes

195 g unsalted butter, softened
125 g (²/₃ cup) soft brown sugar
2 eggs
1 tablespoon coffee and chicory
  essence
155 g (1¼ cups) self-raising flour
100 ml buttermilk
125 g (1 cup) icing sugar

Preheat the oven to 150°C (300°F/ Gas 2). Line two 50 ml 12-hole cupcake trays with paper patty cases. Beat 185 g of the butter and the brown sugar with electric beaters until light and creamy. Add the eggs one at a time, beating well after each addition. Mix in 3 teaspoons of the coffee and chicory essence.

Fold the flour and a pinch of salt alternately with the buttermilk into the creamed mixture until combined. Spoon evenly into the patty cases and bake for 25–30 minutes, or until just springy to the touch. Leave to cool in the tray.

To make the icing, combine the remaining butter, remaining essence, the icing sugar and 1½ tablespoons boiling water in a small bowl. Spread a little icing over each cupcake with a palette knife until evenly covered. If desired, decorate with chocolate-coated coffee beans.

Makes 24

Strawberry cheesecake muffins

250 g (1²/₃ cups) strawberries, hulled
125 g (½ cup) caster sugar
85 g (⅓ cup) cream cheese
1 tablespoon strawberry liqueur
175 g (1⅓ cups) plain flour
1 tablespoon baking powder
1 tablespoon butter, melted
1 teaspoon finely grated orange zest
1 egg
125 ml (½ cup) milk
icing sugar, to dust

Preheat the oven to 180°C (350°F/ Gas 4). Lightly grease six 125 ml (½ cup) non-stick muffin holes with oil. Set aside six small strawberries.

Place half the sugar in a bowl with the cream cheese and mix together well. Place the remaining strawberries in a blender or food processor with the strawberry liqueur and remaining sugar, and blend until smooth. Strain through a fine sieve to remove the strawberry seeds.

Sift the flour and baking powder together in a large bowl and stir in the butter, orange zest and ½ teaspoon salt. In a separate bowl, beat the egg and milk together, then add to the dry ingredients and mix well until combined. Do not overmix.

Spoon half of the mixture into the base of the muffin holes, then add a strawberry and a teaspoon of the cheese mixture. Top with the remaining muffin mixture and bake for 15 minutes, or until cooked and golden. Remove from the tins and cool slightly. Place a muffin on each serving plate, dust with icing sugar and serve drizzled with the sauce.

Makes 6

Desserts

Praline semifreddo

200 g (1¼ cups) blanched almonds
200 g (1 cup) caster sugar
600 ml (2½ cups) thick (double)
  cream
2 eggs, separated
100 g (¾ cup) icing sugar, sifted
2 tablespoons Mandorla (almond-
  flavoured Marsala) or brandy

To make the praline, put the blanched almonds in a hot frying pan and dry-fry until well browned all over, then set aside. Melt the sugar in a saucepan over medium heat until golden, tipping the pan from side to side so the sugar melts evenly. Remove from the heat and stir in the almonds. Carefully pour into a greased baking tray and smooth out with the back of a spoon. Leave to cool completely, then finely crush the praline in a food processor. Pour the cream into a large bowl and whisk until soft peaks form.

Beat the egg yolks with a quarter of the icing sugar until pale. Whisk the egg whites in a clean, dry glass bowl until firm peaks form, then gradually add the rest of the icing sugar and whisk until glossy firm peaks form. Gently fold the egg yolks into the cream, then fold in the egg whites. Fold in the praline and Mandorla.

Line six 250 ml (1 cup) metal dariole moulds with two long strips of foil each, leaving the ends to overhang the edge. Spoon in the mixture, level the surface and tap each mould on the bench. Cover with foil and freeze for 24 hours. To unmould, leave at room temperature for 5 minutes, then lift out with the foil 'handles'.

Serves 6

Peaches cardinal

4 large ripe peaches
300 g (2½ cups) raspberries
2 dessertspoons icing sugar, plus
   extra, to dust

If the peaches are very ripe, put them in a bowl and pour boiling water over them. Leave for a minute, then drain and carefully peel away the skin. If the fruit you have is not so ripe, dissolve 2 tablespoons sugar in a saucepan of water, add the peaches and cover the pan. Gently poach the peaches for 5–10 minutes, or until they are tender. Drain and peel.

Let the peaches cool and then halve each one and remove the stone. Put two halves in each serving glass. Put the raspberries in a food processor or blender and mix until puréed (or mix by hand). Pass through a fine nylon sieve to get rid of the seeds.

Sift the icing sugar over the raspberry purée and stir in. Drizzle the purée over the peaches, cover and chill thoroughly. Dust a little icing sugar over the top to serve.

Serves 4

Watermelon granita

450 g watermelon, skin and seeds
  removed
1 tablespoon liquid glucose or caster
  sugar
1/2 teaspoon lemon juice

Purée the watermelon in a blender
or food processor, or chop it finely
and push it through a metal sieve.
Heat the glucose, lemon juice and
75 ml water in a small saucepan for
4 minutes, or until dissolved. Add the
watermelon and stir well.

Pour into a plastic freezer box, cover
and freeze. Stir every 30 minutes with
a fork during freezing to break up the
ice crystals and give a better texture.
Keep in the freezer until ready to
serve, then roughly fork to break up
the ice crystals.

Serves 4

Baked rice pudding

20 g unsalted butter, melted
3 tablespoons short-grain rice
3 eggs
60 g (¼ cup) caster sugar
440 ml (1¾ cups) milk
125 ml (½ cup) cream
1 teaspoon vanilla essence
¼ teaspoon ground nutmeg

Preheat the oven to 160°C (315°F/ Gas 2–3) and brush a 1.5 litre ovenproof dish with the melted butter. Cook the rice in a saucepan of boiling water for 12 minutes, or until tender, then drain well.

Place the eggs in a bowl and beat lightly. Add the sugar, milk, cream and vanilla essence, and whisk until well combined. Stir in the cooked rice, pour into the prepared dish and sprinkle with nutmeg.

Place the dish in a deep roasting tin and pour enough hot water into the tin to come halfway up the side of the pudding dish. Bake for 45 minutes, or until the custard is lightly set and a knife inserted into the centre comes out clean. Remove the pudding dish from the roasting tin and leave for 5 minutes before serving. Serve the pudding with poached or stewed fruit.

Serves 4–6

Variation: Add 2 tablespoons of sultanas or chopped, dried apricots to the custard mixture before baking.

Blueberry soy cheesecake

250 g wholemeal biscuits
3 teaspoons ground cinnamon
150 g unsalted butter, melted
1½ tablespoons gelatine
250 g silken firm tofu
60 g (¼ cup) caster sugar
250 g (1 cup) cream cheese
300 g vanilla yoghurt
300 g blueberries, or 400 g tinned
    well-drained blueberries, or 300 g
    frozen blueberries, thawed

Preheat the oven to 180°C (350°F/ Gas 4). Grease a 23 cm springform tin.

Place the biscuits and 1 teaspoon of the ground cinnamon in a food processor and blend together until it forms fine crumbs. Transfer to a bowl, add the melted butter and mix well. Press the crumb mixture onto the base of the prepared tin. Bake for 10 minutes, then cool.

Pour 170 ml (⅔ cup) water into a heatproof bowl, evenly sprinkle on the gelatine and leave until spongy — do not stir. Bring a saucepan of water to the boil and remove from the heat. Place the bowl of gelatine in the pan and stir until the gelatine is smooth.

Mix the tofu, sugar, cream cheese and yoghurt in a food processor until smooth. Add the gelatine and process in short bursts for 1–2 seconds.

Place the blueberries on the biscuit base and pour the tofu mixture over the top, spreading evenly. Chill for at least 2 hours. Remove the side of the tin and dust the cheesecake with the remaining ground cinnamon just before serving.

Serves 6–8

Lemon delicious

70 g unsalted butter, at room
  temperature
185 g (¾ cup) sugar
2 teaspoons finely grated lemon zest
3 eggs, separated
30 g (¼ cup) self-raising flour
185 ml (¾ cup) milk
80 ml (⅓ cup) lemon juice
icing sugar, to dust
thick (double) cream, to serve

Preheat the oven to 180°C (350°F/
Gas 4). Melt 10 g of the butter and
use to lightly grease a 1.25 litre
ovenproof ceramic dish.

Using an electric beater, beat the
remaining butter, the sugar and
grated zest together in a bowl until
the mixture is light and creamy.
Gradually add the egg yolks, beating
well after each addition. Fold in the
flour and milk alternately to make
a smooth but runny batter. Stir in
the lemon juice. Don't worry if the
batter looks like it has separated.

Whisk the egg whites in a clean, dry
bowl until firm peaks form and, with a
large metal spoon, fold a third of the
whites into the batter. Gently fold in
the remaining egg whites, being
careful not to overmix.

Pour the batter into the prepared dish
and place in a large roasting tin. Pour
enough hot water into the tin to come
one-third of the way up the side of the
dish and bake for 55 minutes, or until
the top of the pudding is golden,
risen and firm to the touch. Leave for
5 minutes before serving. Dust with
icing sugar and serve with cream.

Serves 4–6

Baklava

560 g (2¼ cups) caster sugar
1½ teaspoons lemon zest
90 g (¼ cup) honey
60 ml (¼ cup) lemon juice
2 tablespoons orange blossom water
200 g (2 cups) walnuts, finely
   chopped
200 g (1⅓ cups) shelled pistachio
   nuts, finely chopped
200 g (1⅓ cups) almonds, finely
   chopped
2 tablespoons caster sugar, extra
2 teaspoons ground cinnamon
375 g filo pastry
200 g unsalted butter, melted

Put the sugar, lemon zest and 375 ml (1½ cups) water in a pan and stir over high heat until the sugar dissolves, then boil for 5 minutes. Reduce the heat and simmer for 5 minutes. Add the honey, lemon juice and orange blossom water and cook for 2 minutes. Remove from the heat and refrigerate.

Preheat the oven to 170°C (325°F/ Gas 3). Combine the nuts, extra sugar and cinnamon. Grease a 30 x 27 cm baking dish. Cover the base with a single layer of filo pastry and brush lightly with melted butter, folding in any overhanging edges. Continue to layer ten more sheets of filo in this manner. Store the remaining filo under a damp tea towel.

Sprinkle half the nuts over the pastry and pat down. Repeat the layering and buttering of five more filo sheets, sprinkle with the rest of the nuts, then layer and butter the remaining filo, brushing the top with butter and pat down. Score into large diamonds. Pour any remaining butter over the top. Bake for 30 minutes, then reduce the heat to 150°C (300°F/Gas 2) and cook for 30 minutes. Immediately cut through the original diamond markings, then strain the syrup over the top. Refrigerate before serving.

Makes 18 pieces

White Christmas

45 g (1½ cups) puffed rice cereal
100 g (1 cup) milk powder
125 g (1 cup) icing sugar
90 g (1 cup) desiccated coconut
80 g (⅓ cup) chopped red glacé
  cherries
80 g (⅓ cup) chopped green glacé
  cherries
55 g (½ cup) sultanas
250 g copha (white vegetable
  shortening)

Line a shallow 28 x 18 cm tin with foil. Put the puffed rice, milk powder, icing sugar, coconut, glacé cherries and sultanas in a large bowl and stir. Make a well in the centre.

Melt the copha over low heat, cool slightly, then add to the well in the puffed rice mixture. Stir with a wooden spoon until all the ingredients are moistened.

Spoon the mixture into the prepared tin and smooth down the surface. Refrigerate for 30 minutes, or until completely set. Remove from the tin, and peel away and discard the foil. Cut into 24 small triangles to serve.

Makes 24 pieces

Chocolate rum mousse

250 g good-quality dark chocolate,
  chopped
3 eggs
60 g (¼ cup) caster sugar
2 teaspoons dark rum
250 ml (1 cup) whipping cream
whipped cream, extra, to serve
dark chocolate, extra, grated, to
  garnish

Put the chocolate in a heatproof bowl. Half fill a saucepan with water and bring to the boil. Remove from the heat and place the bowl over the pan, making sure it is not touching the water. Stir occasionally until the chocolate has melted. Leave to cool.

Using electric beaters, beat the eggs and sugar in a bowl for 5 minutes, or until the mixture is thick, pale and increased in volume. Transfer to a large bowl.

Using a metal spoon, fold in the melted chocolate with the rum, leave the mixture to cool, then gently fold in the lightly whipped cream until just combined.

Spoon into four 250 ml (1 cup) ramekins or dessert glasses. Refrigerate for 2 hours, or until set. Serve with extra whipped cream and garnish with grated chocolate.

Serves 4

Passionfruit soufflé

caster sugar, for lining
40 g unsalted butter
2 tablespoons plain flour
185 ml (³/₄ cup) milk
125 g (½ cup) caster sugar
250 ml (1 cup) fresh passionfruit pulp
  (about 7 large passionfruit)
6 egg whites
icing sugar, to dust

Preheat the oven to 180°C (350°F/ Gas 4). Put an oven tray in the oven to heat. Lightly grease four 300 ml ovenproof ramekins with oil and sprinkle the base and side with caster sugar, shaking out any excess.

Melt the butter in a saucepan over medium heat, add the flour and stir for 1 minute, or until foaming. Remove from the heat and gradually add the milk. Return to the heat and stir constantly for 5–6 minutes, or until the sauce boils and thickens. Reduce the heat and simmer, stirring, for 2 minutes. Transfer to a bowl and stir in the sugar and passionfruit pulp. Do not worry if the mixture looks curdled.

Using electric beaters, beat the egg whites in a clean, dry bowl until firm peaks form. Using a metal spoon, fold a large dollop of the beaten egg white into the passionfruit mixture, then gently fold in the remaining egg white. Make sure you fold the mixture quickly and lightly to incorporate all of the egg white, without losing volume.

Spoon the mixture into the ramekins. Place on the oven tray and bake for 18–20 minutes, or until golden and well risen but still a bit wobbly. Dust with icing sugar and serve immediately.

Serves 4

Fruit poached in red wine

3 pears, peeled, quartered and cored
3 apples, peeled, quartered and
  cored
50 g (¼ cup) sugar
1 vanilla bean, cut in half lengthways
2 small cinnamon sticks
400 ml red wine
200 ml dessert wine or port
700 g red-skinned plums, halved

Put the pears and apples in a large saucepan. Add the sugar, vanilla bean, cinnamon sticks, red wine and dessert wine and bring to the boil. Reduce the heat and gently simmer for 5–10 minutes, or until just soft.

Add the plums, stirring them through the pears and apples, and bring the liquid back to a simmer. Cook for another 5 minutes, or until the plums are soft.

Remove the saucepan from the heat, cover with a lid and leave the fruit to marinate in the syrup for at least 6 hours. Reheat gently to serve warm, or serve at room temperature with cream or ice cream and a biscuit.

Serves 6

Mini éclairs

60 g unsalted butter, chopped
125 g (1 cup) plain flour, sifted
4 eggs, beaten
300 ml (1¼ cups) whipping cream
1 tablespoon icing sugar, sifted
½ teaspoon vanilla essence
50 g dark chocolate, melted (see
  page 390)

Preheat the oven to 200°C (400°F/ Gas 6) and line two baking trays with baking paper. Put the butter in a pan with 250 ml (1 cup) water. Stir over low heat until melted. Bring to the boil, then remove from the heat and add all the flour. Beat with a wooden spoon until smooth. Return to the heat and beat for 2 minutes, or until the mixture forms a ball and leaves the side of the pan. Remove from the heat and transfer to a bowl. Cool for 5 minutes. Add the egg, a little at a time, beating well between each addition, until thick and glossy — a wooden spoon should stand upright.

Spoon the mixture into a piping bag with a 1.2 cm plain nozzle. Pipe 6 cm lengths of batter on the trays. Bake for 10 minutes, then reduce the heat to 180°C (350°F/Gas 4) and cook for 10 minutes, or until golden and puffed. Poke a hole into one side of each éclair and remove the soft dough from inside with a teaspoon. Return to the oven for 2–3 minutes. Cool on a rack.

Whip the cream, icing sugar and vanilla until thick. Pipe the cream into the side of each éclair. Dip each éclair into the melted chocolate, face-side-down, then return to the wire rack for the chocolate to set.

Makes 24

Soy bavarois with mixed berries

2 egg yolks
60 g (¼ cup) caster sugar
185 ml (¾ cup) creamy soy milk
1⅓ gelatine leaves
200 g berry tofu dessert, lightly
  beaten
250 g mixed fresh or frozen berries
  (blackberries, strawberries,
  raspberries, blueberries)
1 tablespoon caster sugar, extra

Lightly grease four 100 ml metal dariole moulds.

Combine the egg yolks and sugar in a heatproof bowl. Heat the milk in a pan over medium heat until almost boiling. Gradually pour onto the egg mixture, stirring constantly. Put the bowl over a pan of simmering water, ensuring the bowl doesn't touch the water, and stir for 10 minutes, or until it thickens and coats the back of a spoon.

Soak the gelatine in cold water for 1 minute, or until softened. Squeeze any excess water from the gelatine, add to the egg mixture, stirring until dissolved. Place the bowl over iced water to chill, and whisk frequently. When cool, gently whisk in the tofu dessert until thoroughly combined. Pour into the moulds and refrigerate for at least 4 hours, or until set.

Put the mixed berries in a saucepan with the extra sugar. Cook, stirring, over low heat for 3–5 minutes, or until the sugar has dissolved. Leave to cool.

To serve, dip the dariole moulds in hot water for 3–5 seconds and turn out onto serving plates. Spoon the mixed berries and syrup around the bavarois and serve.

Serves 4

Coffee granita

200 g (1 cup) caster sugar
1.25 litres (5 cups) very strong
 espresso coffee

Heat the caster sugar with 25 ml hot water in a saucepan until the sugar dissolves. Simmer for 3 minutes to make a sugar syrup. Add the coffee and stir well.

Pour the mixture into a plastic or metal freezer box. The mixture should be no deeper than 3 cm so that the granita freezes quickly and breaks up easily. Stir every 2 hours with a fork to break up the ice crystals as they form. Repeat this two or three times. The granita is ready when almost set but still grainy. Stir a fork through it just before serving.

Serves 6

Rhubarb and berry crumble

850 g rhubarb, cut into 2.5 cm
   lengths
150 g (1¼ cups) blackberries
1 teaspoon grated orange zest
250 g (1 cup) caster sugar
125 g (1 cup) plain flour
115 g (1 cup) ground almonds
½ teaspoon ground ginger
150 g chilled unsalted butter, cubed

Preheat the oven to 180°C (350°F/
Gas 4), and grease a deep 1.5 litre
ovenproof dish. Bring a saucepan of
water to the boil over high heat, add
the rhubarb, and cook for 2 minutes,
or until just tender. Drain well and
combine with the berries, orange zest
and 90 g (⅓ cup) of the caster sugar.
Taste and add a little more sugar if
needed. Spoon the fruit mixture into
the prepared dish.

To make the topping, combine the
flour, ground almonds, ginger and the
remaining sugar. Rub the butter into
the flour mixture with your fingertips
until it resembles coarse breadcrumbs.
Sprinkle the crumble mix over the
fruit, pressing lightly. Don't press it
down too firmly, or it will become flat
and dense.

Put the dish on a baking tray and bake
for 25–30 minutes, or until the topping
is golden and the fruit is bubbling
underneath. Leave for 5 minutes, then
serve with cream or ice cream.

Serves 4

Note: Substitute raspberries,
loganberries or blueberries for the
blackberries. Strawberries do not
work well as they become too soft
when cooked.

Mandarin ice

10 mandarins
125 g (½ cup) caster sugar

Squeeze the mandarins to make 500 ml (2 cups) juice and strain.

Place the sugar and 250 ml (1 cup) water in a small saucepan. Stir over low heat until the sugar has dissolved, then simmer for 5 minutes. Remove from the heat and cool slightly.

Stir the mandarin juice into the sugar syrup, then pour into a shallow metal tray. Freeze for 2 hours, or until frozen. Transfer to a food processor and blend until slushy. Return to the freezer and repeat the process three more times.

Serves 4–6

Cherry clafoutis

500 g fresh cherries (see Hint)
90 g (³/₄ cup) plain flour
2 eggs, lightly beaten
90 g (¹/₃ cup) caster sugar
250 ml (1 cup) milk
60 ml (¹/₄ cup) thick (double) cream
50 g unsalted butter, melted
icing sugar, to dust

Preheat the oven to 180°C (350°F/ Gas 4). Lightly brush a 1.5 litre ovenproof dish with melted butter.

Carefully pit the cherries, then spread into the dish in a single layer.

Sift the flour into a bowl, add the egg and whisk until smooth. Add the caster sugar, milk, cream and butter, whisking until just combined, but being careful not to overbeat.

Pour the batter over the cherries and bake for 30–40 minutes, or until a skewer comes out clean when inserted into the centre. Remove from the oven and dust generously with icing sugar. Serve immediately.

Serves 6–8

Hint: You can use a 720 g jar of cherries. Make sure you thoroughly drain the juice away.
Variation: Blueberries, blackberries, raspberries, or small, well-flavoured strawberries can be used. A delicious version can be made using slices of poached pear.

Self-saucing chocolate pudding

10 g unsalted butter, melted
50 g unsalted butter, chopped, extra
75 g good-quality dark chocolate, chopped
125 ml (½ cup) milk
125 g (1 cup) self-raising flour
4 tablespoons cocoa powder
160 g (¾ cup) caster sugar
1 egg, lightly beaten
115 g (½ cup) firmly packed soft brown sugar
icing sugar, to dust
thick (double) cream or ice cream, to serve

Preheat the oven to 180°C (350°F/ Gas 4) and lightly grease a 2 litre ovenproof dish with the melted butter.

Place the chopped butter, chocolate and milk in a small saucepan, and stir over medium heat for 3–4 minutes, or until the butter and chocolate have melted. Remove the pan from the heat and allow to cool slightly.

Sift the flour and 2 tablespoons of cocoa, and add to the chocolate mixture with the caster sugar and the egg, stirring until just combined. Spoon into the prepared dish.

Sift the remaining cocoa evenly over the top of the pudding and sprinkle with the brown sugar. Pour 560 ml (2¼ cups) boiling water over the back of a spoon (this stops the water making holes in the cake mixture) over the top of the pudding. Bake for 40 minutes, or until the pudding is firm to the touch. Leave for 2 minutes before dusting with icing sugar. Serve with cream or ice cream.

Serves 6

Panna cotta

450 ml (1¾ cups) thick (double)
  cream
4 tablespoons caster sugar
vanilla extract
3 sheets or 1¼ teaspoons gelatine
250 g fresh berries

Put the cream and sugar in a saucepan and stir over gentle heat until the sugar has dissolved. Bring to the boil, then simmer for 3 minutes, adding a few drops of vanilla extract to taste.

If you are using the gelatine sheets, soak in cold water until they are floppy, then squeeze out any excess water. Stir the sheets into the hot cream until they are completely dissolved. If you are using powdered gelatine, sprinkle it onto the hot cream in an even layer and leave it to sponge for a minute, then stir it into the cream until dissolved.

Pour the cream mixture into four 125 ml (½ cup) metal dariole moulds, cover each with plastic wrap and refrigerate until set.

Unmould the panna cotta by wrapping the moulds in a cloth dipped in hot water and tipping them gently onto individual plates. Serve with the fresh berries.

Serves 4

Sticky date puddings

180 g (1 cup) dates, pitted and
  roughly chopped
1 teaspoon bicarbonate of soda
75 g unsalted butter, softened
155 g (²/₃ cup) firmly packed soft
  brown sugar
1 teaspoon vanilla essence
2 eggs
185 g (1½ cups) self-raising flour,
  sifted
100 g (1 cup) walnut halves, roughly
  chopped

Caramel sauce
155 g (²/₃ cup) firmly packed soft
  brown sugar
60 g unsalted butter
250 ml (1 cup) cream

Preheat the oven to 180°C (350°F/
Gas 4). Lightly brush six 250 ml
(1 cup) moulds with melted butter and
line the bases with circles of baking
paper. Put the dates and bicarbonate
of soda in a pan and pour in 250 ml
(1 cup) of water. Bring to the boil,
remove from the heat and set aside to
cool (the mixture will become foamy).

Beat the butter, sugar and vanilla with
electric beaters until light and creamy.
Add 1 egg, beat well and fold through
1 tablespoon of the flour. Add the
other egg and repeat the process.

Fold through the remaining flour,
walnuts and date mixture, and mix
well. Divide the mixture among the
moulds, filling them three-quarters full.
Bake for 30–35 minutes, or until
slightly risen and firm to the touch.

To make the caramel sauce, put the
brown sugar, butter and cream in a
pan and simmer for 5 minutes. When
the puddings are cooked, remove
from the oven and prick a few holes in
each one. Drizzle with some of the
caramel sauce and return to the oven
for 5 minutes. Loosen the side of
each pudding with a small knife, turn
out, remove the baking paper and
serve with the remaining sauce.

Serves 6

Red fruit salad with berries

Syrup
60 g (¼ cup) caster sugar
125 ml (½ cup) dry red wine
1 star anise
1 teaspoon finely chopped lemon zest

250 g (1⅔ cups) strawberries, hulled
  and halved
150 g (1 cup) blueberries
150 g (1¼ cups) raspberries,
  mulberries or other red berries
250 g cherries
5 small red plums (about 250 g),
  stones removed and quartered
yoghurt, to serve

To make the syrup, place the sugar, wine, star anise, lemon zest and 125 ml (½ cup) water in a small saucepan. Bring to the boil over medium heat, stirring to dissolve the sugar. Boil the syrup for 3 minutes, then set aside to cool for 30 minutes. When cool, strain the syrup.

Mix the fruit together in a large bowl and pour on the red wine syrup. Mix well to coat the fruit in the syrup and refrigerate for 1 hour 30 minutes. Serve the fruit dressed with a little syrup and the yoghurt.

Serves 6

Banana fritters in coconut batter

100 g (½ cup) glutinous rice flour
100 g freshly grated coconut or
   60 g desiccated coconut
50 g (¼ cup) sugar
1 tablespoon sesame seeds
60 ml (¼ cup) coconut milk
6 sugar bananas
oil, for deep-frying
ice cream, to serve

Place the flour, coconut, sugar, sesame seeds, coconut milk and 60 ml (¼ cup) water in a bowl and whisk to a smooth batter — add more water if the batter is too thick. Set aside to rest for 1 hour.

Peel the bananas and cut in half lengthways (cut each portion in half crossways if the bananas are large).

Fill a wok or deep heavy-based saucepan one-third full of oil and heat to 180°C (350°F), or until a cube of bread browns in 15 seconds. Dip each piece of banana into the batter, then drop gently into the hot oil. Cook in batches for 4–6 minutes, or until golden brown all over. Remove with a slotted spoon and drain on paper towels. Serve hot with ice cream.

Serves 6

Tipsy strawberry trifle

2 x 85 g packets red jelly crystals
250 ml (1 cup) brandy or rum
250 ml (1 cup) milk
2 x 250 g packets thin sponge finger
  biscuits (savoiardi)
2 x 250 g punnets strawberries,
  hulled and sliced
750 ml (3 cups) ready-made custard
315 ml (1¼ cups) whipping cream

Mix the jelly crystals with 440 ml
(1¾ cups) boiling water and stir to
dissolve. Pour into a shallow tin and
refrigerate until the jelly has just set
but is not firm.

Combine the brandy and milk in a
dish. Dip half the biscuits in the
brandy mixture, then place in a single
layer in a 3 litre glass or ceramic dish.
Spoon half the jelly over the biscuits.
Scatter with half the strawberries and
then pour on half of the custard.

Dip the remaining sponge fingers in
the brandy mixture and place evenly
over the custard, followed by most
of the remaining jelly and custard.
Whip the cream and spread it evenly
over the custard and top with the
remaining strawberries and jelly.
Cover and refrigerate for 4 hours
before serving.

Serves 8

Petits pots de crème

400 ml (1²/₃ cups) milk
1 vanilla bean
3 egg yolks
1 egg
80 g (⅓ cup) caster sugar

Preheat the oven to 140°C (275°F/ Gas 1). Put the milk in a saucepan. Split the vanilla bean in two, scrape out the seeds and add the whole lot to the milk. Bring the milk just to the boil.

Meanwhile, mix together the egg yolks, egg and sugar. Strain the boiling milk over the egg mixture and stir well. Skim off the surface to remove any foam.

Ladle into four 25 ml ramekins and place in a roasting tin. Pour enough hot water into the tin to come halfway up the sides of the ramekins. Bake for 30 minutes, or until the custards are firm to the touch. Leave the ramekins on a wire rack to cool, then refrigerate until ready to serve.

Serves 4

Sticky black rice pudding

400 g (2 cups) black rice
3 fresh pandan leaves
500 ml (2 cups) coconut milk
80 g palm sugar, grated
3 tablespoons caster sugar
coconut cream, to serve
mango or pawpaw cubes, to serve

Place the rice in a large glass or ceramic bowl and cover with water. Leave to soak for at least 8 hours, or preferably overnight. Drain, then place in a saucepan with 1 litre water and slowly bring to the boil. Cook at a low boil, stirring frequently, for 20 minutes, or until tender. Drain.

Pull your fingers through the pandan leaves to shred them and then tie them in a knot. Pour the coconut milk into a large saucepan and heat until almost boiling. Add the palm sugar, caster sugar and pandan leaves and stir until the sugars have dissolved.

Add the rice to the pan and cook, stirring, for 8 minutes without boiling. Turn off the heat, cover and leave for 15 minutes to absorb the flavours. Remove the pandan leaves.

Spoon into bowls and serve warm with coconut cream and fresh mango.

Serves 6–8

Note: Black rice and palm sugar are available from Asian speciality stores. If palm sugar is unavailable, use soft brown sugar.

Baked cheesecake

250 g butternut cookies
1 teaspoon mixed spice
100 g butter, melted
500 g (2 cups) cream cheese,
  softened
160 g ($^3/_4$ cup) caster sugar
4 eggs
1 teaspoon vanilla essence
1 tablespoon orange juice
1 tablespoon grated orange zest

Topping
250 g (1 cup) sour cream
$^1/_2$ teaspoon vanilla essence
3 teaspoons orange juice
1 tablespoon caster sugar
freshly grated nutmeg

Lightly grease the base of a 20 cm springform tin.

Finely crush the biscuits in a food processor for 30 seconds, or put them in a plastic bag and roll with a rolling pin. Transfer to a bowl and add the mixed spice and butter. Stir until all the crumbs are moistened, then spoon the mixture into the tin and press it firmly into the base and side. Refrigerate for 20 minutes, or until firm.

Preheat the oven to 180°C (350°F/ Gas 4). Beat the cream cheese until smooth. Add the sugar and beat until smooth. Add the eggs, one at a time, beating well after each addition. Mix in the vanilla, orange juice and zest.

Pour the mixture into the crumb case and bake for 45 minutes, or until just firm. To make the topping, combine the sour cream, vanilla, orange juice and sugar in a bowl. Spread over the hot cheesecake, sprinkle with nutmeg and return to the oven for 7 minutes. Cool, then refrigerate until firm.

Serves 8

Desserts

Lemon gelato

5 egg yolks
125 g (½ cup) sugar
500 ml (2 cups) milk
2 tablespoons grated lemon zest
185 ml (¾ cup) lemon juice
3 tablespoons thick (double) cream

Whisk the egg yolks and half the sugar together until pale and creamy. Put the milk, lemon zest and remaining sugar in a saucepan and bring to the boil. Pour over the egg mixture and whisk to combine.

Pour the custard back into the saucepan and cook over low heat, stirring continuously until the mixture is thick enough to coat the back of a wooden spoon — do not allow the custard to boil. Strain the custard into a bowl, add the lemon juice and cream and then cool over ice.

Churn in an ice-cream maker following the manufacturer's instructions. Or, pour into a plastic freezer box, cover and freeze. Stir every 30 minutes with a whisk during freezing to break up the ice crystals and give a better texture. Keep in the freezer until ready to serve.

Serves 6

Apple sago pudding

90 g (1/3 cup) caster sugar
100 g (1/2 cup) sago
600 ml (2 1/2 cups) milk
55 g (1/2 cup) sultanas
1 teaspoon vanilla essence
pinch ground nutmeg
1/4 teaspoon ground cinnamon
2 eggs, lightly beaten
3 small ripe apples (about 250 g),
   peeled, cored and very thinly sliced
1 tablespoon soft brown sugar

Preheat the oven to 180°C (350°F/
Gas 4). Grease a 1.5 litre ceramic
soufflé dish. Place the sugar, sago,
milk, sultanas and 1/4 teaspoon salt in
a saucepan and heat, stirring often.
Bring to the boil, then reduce the heat
and simmer for 5 minutes.

Stir in the vanilla essence, nutmeg,
cinnamon, egg and the apple slices,
then pour into the prepared dish.
Sprinkle with the brown sugar and
bake for 45 minutes, or until set and
golden brown.

Serves 4

Passionfruit mousse

5–6 passionfruit
6 eggs, separated
185 g (³/₄ cup) caster sugar
¹/₂ teaspoon finely grated lemon zest
3 tablespoons lemon juice
1 tablespoon gelatine
315 ml (1¹/₄ cups) whipping cream,
   lightly whipped
40 g (³/₄ cup) flaked or shredded
   (²/₃ cup) coconut, toasted

Cut the passionfruit in half and scoop out the pulp. Strain, then measure out 3 tablespoons of juice and set aside. Add the seeds and pulp to the remaining juice and set aside. Put the egg yolks, 125 g (¹/₂ cup) of the sugar, lemon zest, lemon juice and strained passionfruit juice in a heatproof bowl. Put the bowl over a pan of simmering water and, using electric beaters, beat for 10 minutes, or until thick and creamy. Remove from the heat and transfer to a glass bowl.

Sprinkle the gelatine over 125 ml (¹/₂ cup) water in a small bowl and leave until spongy. Put the bowl in a pan of just-boiled water (the water should come halfway up the bowl) and stir until dissolved. Add the gelatine to the mousse mixture and mix well. Mix in the passionfruit pulp and leave until cold, then fold in the whipped cream.

Using electric beaters, whisk the egg whites until soft peaks form. Gradually whisk in the remaining sugar, beating until the sugar has dissolved. Fold the egg whites into the mousse mixture quickly and lightly. Spoon into eight 250 ml (1 cup) ramekins or stemmed wine glasses. Refrigerate for 2 hours, or until set. Sprinkle with the coconut just before serving.

Serves 10–12

Plum cobbler

825 g tin dark plums, pitted
1 tablespoon honey
2 ripe pears, peeled, cored and cut
    into eighths

Topping
250 g (1 cup) self-raising flour
1 tablespoon caster sugar
1/4 teaspoon ground cardamom or
    ground cinnamon
40 g unsalted butter, chilled and
    chopped
60 ml (1/4 cup) milk
extra milk, for brushing
1 tablespoon caster sugar, extra
1/4 teaspoon ground cardamom or
    ground cinnamon, extra

Preheat the oven to 200°C (400°F/
Gas 6). Grease an 18 cm round
(1.5 litre) ovenproof dish. Drain the
plums, reserving 185 ml (3/4 cup) of
the syrup. Place the syrup, honey and
pear in a large wide saucepan and
bring to the boil. Reduce the heat and
simmer for 8 minutes, or until the pear
is tender. Add the plums.

To make the topping, sift the flour,
sugar, cardamom and a pinch of salt
into a large bowl. Rub in the butter
with your fingers until it resembles fine
breadcrumbs. Stir in the milk using a
flat-bladed knife, mixing lightly to form
a soft dough — add a little more milk
if necessary. Turn onto a lightly floured
surface and form into a smooth ball.
Roll out to a 1 cm thickness and cut
into rounds with a 4 cm cutter.

Spoon the hot fruit into the dish, then
arrange the circles of dough in an
overlapping pattern over the fruit, on
the inside edge of the dish only —
leave the fruit in the centre exposed.
Brush the dough with the extra milk.
Mix the extra sugar and cardamom
and sprinkle over the dough.

Place the dish on a baking tray and
bake for 30 minutes, or until the
topping is golden and cooked.

Serves 4

Cinnamon orange mini pavlovas with berries

2 egg whites
125 g (½ cup) caster sugar
2 teaspoons ground cinnamon
1 teaspoon finely grated orange zest
3 teaspoons cornflour
1 teaspoon white vinegar
125 ml (½ cup) whipping cream
fresh berries

Preheat the oven to 140°C (275°F/ Gas 1). Line a baking tray with baking paper and mark four 10 cm circles. Turn the baking paper upside down so the marks don't stain the meringue.

Beat the egg whites with electric beaters until soft peaks form. Gradually add the sugar, beating well after each addition. Continue to beat for 4–5 minutes, or until the sugar has dissolved and the meringue is thick and glossy. Gently fold in the cinnamon, orange zest, cornflour and vinegar. Place 2 tablespoons of the mixture into each circle, gently spreading it out to the edges with the back of a spoon. Hollow out each centre to make nest shapes.

Bake for 10 minutes, then turn the tray around and bake for a further 30–35 minutes, or until the pavlovas are pale and crisp. Turn the oven off and leave them to cool completely with the door slightly ajar. The pavlovas may crack slightly on cooling. Whip the cream and spoon a little into each pavlova, top with the berries and serve immediately.

Serves 4

Zabaglione

6 egg yolks
3 tablespoons caster sugar
125 ml (½ cup) sweet Marsala
250 ml (1 cup) thick (double) cream

Whisk the egg yolks and sugar in the top of a double boiler or in a heatproof bowl set over a saucepan of simmering water. Make sure that the water does not touch the base of the bowl or the egg may overcook and stick. It is important that you whisk constantly to move the cooked mixture from the outside of the bowl to the centre.

When the egg mixture is tepid, add the Marsala and whisk for another 5 minutes, or until it has thickened enough to hold its shape when drizzled off the whisk into the bowl.

Whip the cream until soft peaks form. Gently fold in the egg and Marsala mixture. Divide among four glasses or bowls. Cover and refrigerate for 3–4 hours before serving.

Serves 4

Bread and butter pudding

2 tablespoons sultanas
1 tablespoon Grand Marnier
10 slices day-old white bread, crusts
   removed
2½ tablespoons marmalade
2 eggs
2 tablespoons caster sugar
500 ml (2 cups) milk
1 teaspoon vanilla essence

Place the sultanas in a bowl, add the Grand Marnier, toss to coat and leave for 30 minutes. Preheat the oven to 160°C (315°F/Gas 2–3).

Spread the slices of bread with 1½ tablespoons of the marmalade. Cut each slice into four triangles. Lightly grease a 1.5 litre ovenproof dish with oil. Layer the bread in the dish, sprinkling the sultanas between the layers.

Whisk the eggs, sugar, milk and vanilla essence together in a bowl. Pour over the bread and leave to soak for at least 30 minutes.

Place the pudding dish in a large roasting tin and pour in boiling water to come halfway up the side of the pudding dish, then bake in the oven for 35–40 minutes. Remove the pudding dish from the roasting tin and brush with the remaining marmalade. Leave for 10 minutes, then serve.

Serves 6

Amaretti-stuffed peaches

6 ripe peaches
60 g amaretti biscuits, crushed
1 egg yolk
2 tablespoons caster sugar
20 g (¼ cup) ground almonds
1 tablespoon amaretto
60 ml (¼ cup) white wine
1 teaspoon caster sugar, extra
20 g unsalted butter

Preheat the oven to 180°C (350°F/ Gas 4) and lightly grease a 30 x 25 cm ovenproof dish with butter.

Cut each peach in half and carefully remove the stones. Scoop a little of the pulp out from each and combine in a small bowl with the crushed biscuits, egg yolk, caster sugar, ground almonds and amaretto.

Spoon some of the mixture into each peach and place them cut-side-up in the dish. Sprinkle with the white wine and the extra sugar. Put a dot of butter on the top of each and bake for 20–25 minutes, or until golden.

Serves 6

Note: When they are in season, you can also use ripe apricots or nectarines for this recipe.

Apricot honey soufflé

180 g (1 cup) dried whole apricots,
  chopped
2 tablespoons caster sugar
2 egg yolks
1½ tablespoons honey, warmed
1 teaspoon finely grated lemon zest
4 egg whites
icing sugar, to dust

Place the apricots in a saucepan with 125 ml (½ cup) cold water, or enough to cover. Bring to the boil, then reduce the heat and simmer for 20 minutes, or until the apricots are soft and pulpy. Drain, then process in a food processor to a purée.

Preheat the oven to 200°C (400°F/ Gas 6). Lightly grease a 1.25 litre soufflé dish and sprinkle the base and side with 1 tablespoon of caster sugar. Put the egg yolks, honey, zest and apricot purée in a bowl and beat until smooth.

Whisk the egg whites in a clean, dry bowl until soft peaks form, then whisk in the remaining sugar. Fold 1 tablespoon into the apricot mixture and mix well. Lightly fold in the remaining egg white, being careful to keep the mixture light and aerated. Spoon into the soufflé dish and level the surface. Run your thumb around the inside rim to create a gap between the mixture and the wall of the dish (this will encourage even rising).

Bake on the upper shelf in the oven for 25–30 minutes, or until risen and just set. Cover loosely with foil if the surface starts to overbrown. Dust with icing sugar and serve.

Serves 4

Nougat

500 g (2 cups) sugar
250 ml (1 cup) liquid glucose
175 g (½ cup) honey (preferably
  blossom honey)
2 egg whites
1 teaspoon vanilla essence
125 g unsalted butter, softened
60 g (⅓ cup) almonds, unblanched
  and toasted
100 g (½ cup) glacé cherries (not
  imitation)

Grease a 28 x 18 cm baking dish and line with baking paper. Place the sugar, glucose, honey, 60 ml (¼ cup) water and ¼ teaspoon salt in a heavy-based pan and stir over low heat until dissolved. Boil for 8 minutes, or until the mixture reaches hard ball stage (see page 393) or 121°C (250°F) on the sugar thermometer.

Beat the egg whites in a bowl with electric beaters until firm peaks form. Slowly pour a quarter of the syrup onto the egg whites in a thin stream and beat for up to 5 minutes, or until the mixture holds its shape. Place the remaining syrup over the heat and cook for 2 minutes, or until it reaches hard crack stage (see page 393), or 143°C (290°F) on the thermometer. Pour slowly onto the meringue mixture with the beaters running and beat until very thick.

Add the vanilla and butter and beat for 5 minutes. Stir in the almonds and cherries using a metal spoon. Turn the mixture into the tin and smooth the top with a palette knife. Refrigerate for at least 4 hours, or until firm. Cut into pieces with a very sharp knife. Wrap each piece in cellophane and store in the refrigerator.

Makes 1 kg

Grilled figs with ricotta

2 tablespoons honey
1 cinnamon stick
3 tablespoons flaked almonds
4 large (or 8 small) fresh figs
125 g (½ cup) ricotta cheese
½ teaspoon vanilla essence
2 tablespoons icing sugar, sifted
pinch ground cinnamon
½ teaspoon finely grated orange zest

Place the honey and cinnamon stick in a small saucepan with 80 ml (⅓ cup) water. Bring to the boil, then reduce the heat and simmer gently for 6 minutes, or until thickened and reduced by half. Discard the cinnamon stick and stir in the almonds.

Preheat the grill to moderately hot and grease a shallow ovenproof dish large enough to fit all the figs side by side. Slice the figs into quarters from the top to within 1 cm of the bottom, keeping them attached at the base. Arrange in the prepared dish.

Combine the ricotta, vanilla, icing sugar, ground cinnamon and orange zest in a small bowl. Divide the filling among the figs, spooning it into their cavities. Spoon the syrup over the top. Place under the grill and cook until the juices start to come out from the figs and the almonds are lightly toasted. Cool for 2–3 minutes. Spoon the juices and any fallen almonds from the bottom of the dish over the figs and serve.

Serves 4

Baked custard

10 g unsalted butter, melted
3 eggs
90 g (⅓ cup) caster sugar
500 ml (2 cups) milk
125 ml (½ cup) cream
1½ teaspoons vanilla essence
ground nutmeg

Preheat the oven to 160°C (315°F/ Gas 2–3) and brush four 250 ml (1 cup) ramekins or a 1.5 litre ovenproof dish with the melted butter.

Whisk together the eggs and sugar in a large bowl until they are combined. Place the milk and cream in a small saucepan and stir over medium heat for 3–4 minutes, or until the mixture is warmed through, then stir into the egg mixture with the vanilla essence. Strain into the prepared dishes and sprinkle with the ground nutmeg.

Place the dishes in a deep roasting tin and add enough hot water to come halfway up the side of the dishes. Bake for 25 minutes for the individual custards, or 30 minutes for the large custard, or until it is set and a knife inserted into the centre comes out clean.

Remove the custards from the roasting tin and leave for 10 minutes before serving.

Serves 4

Variation: Omit the vanilla and add 1½ tablespoons of Amaretto or Grand Marnier liqueur to the custard before baking.

Crème caramel

250 ml (1 cup) milk
250 ml (1 cup) cream
375 g (1 1/2 cups) caster sugar
1 teaspoon vanilla essence
4 eggs, lightly beaten
90 g (1/3 cup) caster sugar, extra

Preheat the oven to 200°C (400°F/ Gas 6). Place the milk and cream in a saucepan and gradually bring to boiling point.

Put the sugar in a frying pan and cook over medium heat for 8–10 minutes. Stir occasionally as the sugar melts to form a golden toffee. The sugar may clump together — break up any lumps with a wooden spoon. Pour the toffee into the base of six 125 ml (1/2 cup) ramekins or ovenproof dishes.

Combine the vanilla, eggs and extra sugar in a bowl. Remove the milk and cream from the heat and gradually add to the egg mixture, whisking well. Pour the custard mixture evenly over the toffee. Place the ramekins in a baking dish and pour in boiling water until it comes halfway up the sides of the dishes. Bake for 20 minutes, or until set. Use a flat-bladed knife to run around the edges of the dishes and carefully turn out the crème caramel onto a serving plate, toffee-side-up.

Serves 6

Note: When making toffee, watch it carefully as it will take a little while to start melting, but once it starts it will happen very quickly. Stir occasionally to make sure it melts evenly and doesn't stick to the saucepan.

Chocolate fudge puddings

150 g unsalted butter
185 g (³/4 cup) caster sugar
100 g dark chocolate, melted
  and cooled (see page 390)
2 eggs
60 g (¹/2 cup) plain flour
125 g (1 cup) self-raising flour
30 g (¹/4 cup) cocoa powder
1 teaspoon bicarbonate of soda
125 ml (¹/2 cup) milk

Sauce
50 g unsalted butter, chopped
125 g dark chocolate, chopped
125 ml (¹/2 cup) cream
1 teaspoon vanilla essence

Preheat the oven to 180°C (350°F/ Gas 4). Lightly grease eight 250 ml (1 cup) metal moulds with melted butter and line each base with a round of baking paper.

Beat the butter and caster sugar until light and creamy. Add the melted chocolate, beating well. Add the eggs one at a time, beating well after each addition.

Sift together the plain and self-raising flours, cocoa powder and bicarbonate of soda, then fold into the chocolate mixture. Add the milk and fold through. Half fill the moulds. Cover the moulds with pieces of greased foil and place in a large, deep baking dish. Pour in enough boiling water to come halfway up the sides of the moulds. Bake for 35–40 minutes, or until a skewer inserted into the centre of each pudding comes out clean.

To make the sauce, combine the butter, chocolate, cream and vanilla in a pan. Stir over low heat until the butter and chocolate have completely melted. Pour over the pudding and serve with whipped cream.

Serves 8

Crepes with warm fruit compote

Crepes
60 g (½ cup) plain flour
2 eggs
250 ml (1 cup) milk
2 teaspoons caster sugar

Compote
100 g (½ cup) whole dried apricots
60 ml (¼ cup) port or Muscat
1 vanilla bean, halved
2 firm pears, peeled, cored and
   quartered
2 cinnamon sticks
425 g tin pitted prunes in syrup,
   drained, syrup reserved

Place the flour in a bowl and gradually add the combined eggs and milk, whisking to remove any lumps. Cover the batter with plastic wrap and leave for 30 minutes.

To make the compote, put the apricots and port in a pan and cook, covered, over low heat for 2–3 minutes, or until softened. Scrape the seeds from the vanilla bean and add both the seeds and vanilla bean to the pan along with the pear, cinnamon and prune syrup. Simmer, covered, stirring occasionally, for 4 minutes, or until the pear has softened. Add the prunes and simmer for 1 minute.

Heat a 20 cm non-stick crepe pan or frying pan over medium heat. Lightly grease with oil. Pour 60 ml (¼ cup) of batter into the pan and swirl evenly over the base. Cook each crepe for 1 minute, or until the underside is golden. Turn it over and cook the other side for 30 seconds, then remove. Keep warm and repeat to make eight crepes.

Fold the crepes into triangles and scatter with caster sugar. Serve with the compote.

Serves 4

Apricots in cardamom syrup

300 g (1²/₃ cups) dried apricots
3 tablespoons caster sugar
3 tablespoons slivered, blanched
   almonds
1 cm piece of ginger, sliced
4 cardamom pods
1 cinnamon stick
4 pieces edible silver leaf (varak),
   optional

Soak the apricots in 750 ml (3 cups) water in a large saucepan for 4 hours, or until plumped up.

Add the caster sugar, almonds, ginger, cardamom and cinnamon to the apricots and bring slowly to the boil, stirring until the sugar has dissolved. Reduce the heat to a simmer and cook until the liquid has reduced by half and formed a thick syrup. Pour into a bowl, then refrigerate.

Serve in small bowls with a piece of silver leaf for decoration. To do this, invert the piece of backing paper over each bowl. As soon as the silver leaf touches the apricots it will come away from the backing and stick to them.

Serves 4

Zuppa inglese

Custard
6 large egg yolks
100 g (½ cup) caster sugar
2 tablespoons cornflour
1 tablespoon plain flour
600 ml (2½ cups) milk
½ vanilla bean or 1 teaspoon vanilla
  extract

1 ready-made sponge cake
150 ml (⅔ cup) clear alcohol, such as
  grappa or kirsch
200 g (1⅔ cups) raspberries
350 g (3 cups) blackberries
2 teaspoons caster sugar
250 ml (1 cup) whipping cream

To make the custard, whisk the egg yolks with the sugar until pale and fluffy. Add the cornflour and flour and mix well. Heat the milk with the vanilla bean and bring just to the boil. Pour into the egg mixture, whisking as you do so. Pour back into the saucepan and gently bring to the boil, stirring all the time. Once the mixture is just boiling, take it off the heat and stir for another few minutes. Pour into a bowl and cover the surface with plastic wrap to prevent a skin forming.

Slice the sponge into 2 cm strips. Place a couple of pieces on each plate (you need to use deep plates) and brush with about 100 ml of the alcohol. Leave to soak for at least 10 minutes.

Put the raspberries and blackberries in a saucepan with the remaining alcohol and the caster sugar. Gently warm through so that the sugar just melts, then set aside to cool. Spoon over the sponge, then pour the custard over the top of the fruit. Lightly whip the cream and serve on the side.

Serves 6

Caramelized apple mousse

50 g unsalted butter
60 g (¼ cup) caster sugar
170 ml (⅔ cup) whipping cream
500 g green apples, peeled, cored
  and cut into thin wedges
2 eggs, separated

Place the butter and sugar in a frying pan and stir over low heat until the sugar has dissolved. Increase the heat to medium and cook until the mixture turns deeply golden, stirring frequently. Add 2 tablespoons of the cream and stir to remelt the caramel.

Add the apple wedges and cook, stirring frequently, over medium heat for 10–15 minutes, or until caramelized. Remove eight apple wedges and set aside to use as garnish.

Blend the remaining apples and caramel in a food processor until smooth. Transfer to a large bowl, then stir in the egg yolks and leave to cool.

Whisk the egg whites in a clean, dry bowl until soft peaks form, then fold into the cooled apple mixture. Whip the remaining cream until firm peaks form and fold into the apple mixture. Pour into a 750 ml (3 cup) serving bowl or four 185 ml (¾ cup) individual serving moulds. Refrigerate for 3 hours, or until firm. Serve with the reserved apple wedges.

Serves 4

Caramel ice cream

70 g (⅓ cup) sugar
80 ml (⅓ cup) cream
3 egg yolks
360 ml (1½ cups) milk
1 vanilla bean

To make the caramel, put 45 g of the sugar in a heavy-based saucepan and heat until it dissolves and starts to caramelize — tip the saucepan from side to side as the sugar cooks to keep the colouring even. Remove from the heat and carefully add the cream (it will splutter). Stir over low heat until the caramel remelts.

Whisk the egg yolks and remaining sugar until light and fluffy. Put the milk and vanilla bean in a saucepan and bring just to the boil, then strain over the caramel. Bring back to the boil and pour over the egg yolk mixture, whisking continuously.

Pour the custard back into the pan and cook, stirring, until it is thick enough to coat the back of a wooden spoon. Do not let it boil or it will split. Pass through a sieve into a bowl and leave over ice to cool quickly.

Churn in an ice-cream maker following the manufacturer's instructions. Or, pour into a plastic freezer box, cover and freeze. Stir every 30 minutes with a whisk during freezing to break up the ice crystals. Freeze overnight with a layer of plastic wrap over the surface and the lid on the container. Keep in the freezer until ready to serve.

Serves 4

White chocolate cheesecakes with mixed berries

4 butternut biscuits
75 g (1/2 cup) good-quality white chocolate bits (chocolate chips)
250 g (1 cup) cream cheese, at room temperature
60 ml (1/4 cup) whipping cream
125 g (1/2 cup) caster sugar
1 egg
250 g (1 1/2–2 cups) mixed berries, such as raspberries, blueberries and sliced strawberries
Framboise or Cointreau, optional

Preheat the oven to 160°C (315°F/ Gas 2–3). Grease four 250 ml (1 cup) muffin holes and line with 2 strips of baking paper to make a cross pattern. Put a biscuit in the base of each hole. Put the chocolate bits in a heatproof bowl. Bring a saucepan of water to the boil, then remove from the heat. Sit the bowl over the pan, making sure the base of the bowl does not sit in the water. Stir occasionally until the chocolate has melted.

Using electric beaters, beat the cream cheese, cream and half the sugar until thick and smooth. Beat in the egg and then the melted chocolate. Pour evenly into the muffin holes and bake for 25 minutes, or until set. Cool completely in the tin, then carefully run a small spatula or flat-bladed knife around the edge and lift out of the holes using the paper strips as handles. Refrigerate for 1 hour, or until ready to serve.

Place the berries in a bowl and fold in the remaining sugar. Leave for 10–15 minutes, or until juices form. Flavour with a little liqueur, such as Framboise or Cointreau, if desired. Serve the cheesecakes on individual serving plates topped with the berries.

Serves 4

Cinnamon gelato

1 vanilla bean
550 ml (2¼ cups) thick (double)
   cream
550 ml (2¼ cups) milk
2 cinnamon sticks
6 egg yolks
100 g (½ cup) caster sugar

Split the vanilla bean down the middle, leaving it joined at one end, and put it in a saucepan with the cream, milk and cinnamon sticks. Bring just to the boil, then remove from the heat and leave to infuse for 1 hour.

Whisk the egg yolks and sugar in a large bowl until pale and creamy. Pour the milk over the egg yolk mixture and whisk quickly to combine. Pour the custard back into the saucepan and cook over very low heat to just thicken it, stirring continuously with a wooden spoon. Remove from the heat and dip the spoon into the custard. Draw a line on the back of the spoon — if the line stays and the custard does not run through it, then it is ready; if not, cook a little longer. Do not allow the custard to boil.

Scrape out the vanilla seeds and mix them into the custard. Strain into a bowl, removing the vanilla bean and cinnamon sticks, and leave to cool. Churn in an ice-cream maker following the manufacturer's instructions. Or, pour into a metal or plastic freezer box and freeze, whisking every 30 minutes to break up the ice crystals and give a creamy texture. Once set, keep in the freezer until ready to serve.

Serves 8

Coffee crémets with chocolate sauce

250 g (1 cup) cream cheese
250 ml (1 cup) thick (double) cream
4 tablespoons very strong coffee
80 g (⅓ cup) caster sugar

Chocolate sauce
100 g dark chocolate
50 g unsalted butter

Line four 100 ml ramekins or heart-shaped moulds with muslin, leaving enough muslin hanging over the side to wrap over the crémet.

Beat the cream cheese a little until smooth, then whisk in the cream. Add the coffee and sugar and mix. Spoon into the ramekins and fold the muslin over the top. Refrigerate for at least 1 hour 30 minutes, then unwrap the muslin and turn the crémets out onto individual plates, carefully peeling the muslin off each one.

To make the chocolate sauce, gently melt the chocolate in a saucepan with the butter and 4 tablespoons water. Stir well to make a shiny sauce, then let the sauce cool a little. Pour a little chocolate sauce over each crémet.

Serves 4

Note: Dark chocolate (also known as plain or bittersweet) is available with different amounts of added sugar. For a really good chocolate sauce, you want to use chocolate with less sugar and more cocoa solids (between 50% and 70%).

Pistachio crème brûlée

500 ml (2 cups) cream
35 g (¼ cup) finely chopped
  pistachios
½ vanilla bean, halved lengthways
½ teaspoon grated orange zest
100 g (½ cup) caster sugar
5 egg yolks
1–3 tablespoons caster sugar, extra
pistachio biscotti, to serve

Preheat the oven to 140°C (275°F/ Gas 1). Put the cream, pistachios, vanilla bean, zest and half the sugar in a saucepan over medium heat and stir to dissolve the sugar, then slowly bring to the boil. Remove from the heat and infuse for 10 minutes.

Whisk the egg yolks and remaining sugar in a bowl. Strain the cream mixture into a jug, then add to the egg mixture, stirring continuously. Ladle the custard into six ½ cup (125 ml) ramekins and place in a roasting tin. Pour in cold water to come halfway up the sides of the ramekins, then place in the oven and cook for 1 hour, or until the custard has set and is only just wobbly. Cool the ramekins on a wire rack, then refrigerate for 4 hours.

Preheat the grill to very hot. Sprinkle 1–2 teaspoons of the extra sugar over the top of each brûlée. Put the brûlées in a roasting tin full of ice, then put the tin under the grill for 4 minutes, or until the tops of the brûlées have melted and caramelized. Remove the ramekins from the roasting tin and dry around the outside edges. Refrigerate for 1–2 hours but not more than 3 hours (or the toffee will start to go sticky and lose its crunch). Serve with pistachio biscotti and some fresh fruit.

Serves 6

Pies & Tarts

Chocolate and peanut butter pie

200 g chocolate biscuits with cream
  centre, crushed
50 g unsalted butter, melted
200 g ($^3/_4$ cup) cream cheese
85 g ($^2/_3$ cup) icing sugar, sifted
100 g ($^2/_3$ cup) smooth peanut butter
1 teaspoon vanilla essence
250 ml (1 cup) whipping cream,
  whipped to firm peaks
60 ml ($^1/_4$ cup) cream, extra
3 teaspoons unsalted butter, extra
50 g dark chocolate, grated
honey-roasted peanuts, chopped, to
  garnish

Combine the biscuit crumbs with the melted butter and press into the base and side of a deep 23 cm (top) 18 cm (base) 3 cm (deep) pie dish and refrigerate for 15 minutes, or until firm.

Put the cream cheese and icing sugar in a bowl and beat with electric beaters until smooth. Add the peanut butter and vanilla and beat together. Stir in a third of the whipped cream until smooth, then gently fold in the remaining whipped cream. Pour the mixture into the pie shell. Refrigerate for 2 hours, or until firm.

Place the extra cream and butter in a pan and stir over medium heat until the butter is melted and the cream just comes to a simmer. Remove from the heat, add the grated chocolate, and stir until melted. Cool a little, then dribble the chocolate over the top of the pie to create a lattice pattern. Refrigerate for 2 hours, or until the topping and chocolate are firm.

Remove the pie from the fridge, scatter over the chopped peanuts and serve.

Serves 10–12

Individual lemon and passionfruit tarts with raspberries

60 g unsalted butter
90 g (⅓ cup) caster sugar
2 eggs
2 tablespoons self-raising flour, sifted
60 ml (¼ cup) lemon juice
1 teaspoon grated lemon zest
1 passionfruit, pulp removed
3 sheets filo pastry
125 g (1 cup) fresh raspberries

Preheat the oven to 180°C (350°F/ Gas 4). Beat the butter and caster sugar until light and creamy. Add the eggs one at a time, beating well after each addition. Add the flour, lemon juice, zest and passionfruit pulp and beat until well combined.

Fold each sheet of filo pastry in half from the short end up. Fold again and cut in half. Carefully line six 125 ml (½ cup) muffin holes with a piece of pastry. Pour in the lemon mixture and bake for 20–25 minutes, or until set.

Serve topped with fresh raspberries and, if desired, whipped cream.

Makes 6

Freeform blueberry pie

Pastry
185 g (1 1/2 cups) plain flour
100 g unsalted butter, chilled and
  cubed
2 teaspoons grated orange zest
1 tablespoon caster sugar
2–3 tablespoons iced water

40 g (1/3 cup) crushed amaretti
  biscuits or almond bread
60 g (1/2 cup) plain flour
1 teaspoon ground cinnamon
90 g (1/3 cup) caster sugar
500 g (3 1/4 cups) fresh blueberries
milk, for brushing
2 tablespoons blueberry jam
icing sugar, to dust

Sift the flour into a large bowl and rub in the butter with your fingertips until the mixture resembles breadcrumbs. Stir in the orange zest and sugar. Make a well, add almost all the water and mix with a flat-bladed knife, using a cutting action, until the mixture comes together in beads. Add a little more water if necessary to bring the dough together. Gather together and lift out onto a lightly floured surface. Press together into a ball and flatten it slightly into a disc. Cover in plastic wrap and refrigerate for 20 minutes.

Preheat the oven to 200°C (400°F/ Gas 6). Combine the crushed biscuits, flour, cinnamon and 1 1/2 tablespoons of the sugar. Roll the pastry out to a 36 cm circle and sprinkle with the biscuit mixture, leaving a 4 cm border. Arrange the blueberries over the crushed biscuits, then bring up the edges to form a freeform crust.

Brush the sides of the pie with the milk. Sprinkle with the remaining sugar and bake for 30 minutes, or until the sides are crisp and brown.

Warm the jam in a saucepan over low heat and brush over the berries. Cool to room temperature, then dust the pastry crust with sifted icing sugar.

Serves 6–8

Rhubarb pie

Pastry
250 g (2 cups) plain flour
30 g unsalted butter, chilled and
  cubed
70 g copha (white vegetable
  shortening)
2 tablespoons icing sugar
160 ml (²/₃ cup) iced water

1.5 kg rhubarb, trimmed and cut into
  2 cm pieces
250 g (1 cup) caster sugar
½ teaspoon ground cinnamon
2½ tablespoons cornflour, mixed with
  60 ml (¼ cup) water
30 g unsalted butter, cubed
1 egg, lightly beaten
icing sugar, to dust

Grease a 25 x 20 x 4 cm ceramic pie dish. Sift the flour and ½ teaspoon salt into a bowl and rub in the butter and copha until the mixture looks like breadcrumbs. Stir in the icing sugar. Make a well, add most of the water and mix with a flat-bladed knife, using a cutting action, until it comes together in beads. Add more water if needed. Gather the dough together and put on a floured surface. Press into a ball, flatten a little and cover in plastic wrap. Refrigerate for 30 minutes.

Put the rhubarb, sugar, cinnamon and 2 tablespoons water in a pan and stir over low heat until the sugar dissolves. Simmer, covered, for 5–8 minutes, or until the rhubarb is tender. Add the cornflour and water mixture. Bring to the boil, stirring until thickened. Cool. Preheat the oven to 180°C (350°F/ Gas 4) and heat a baking tray.

Roll out two-thirds of the dough to a 30 cm circle and put into the pie dish. Spoon in the rhubarb and dot with butter. Roll out the remaining pastry for a lid. Brush the pie rim with egg and press the top in place. Trim the edges and make a slit in the top. Decorate with pastry scraps and brush with egg. Bake on the hot tray for 35 minutes, or until golden. Dust with icing sugar.

Serves 6

Mixed berry tartlets

Pastry
350 g (2³/₄ cups) plain flour
small pinch of salt
150 g unsalted butter
100 g (³/₄ cup) icing sugar
2 eggs, beaten

Frangipane
250 g unsalted butter, softened
250 g (2 cups) icing sugar
250 g (2¹/₂ cups) ground almonds
40 g (¹/₃ cup) plain flour
5 eggs, lightly beaten

400 g mixed berries
3 tablespoons apricot jam

To make the pastry, sift the flour and salt onto a work surface and make a well in the centre. Put the butter into the well and work, using a pecking action with your fingertips and thumb, until it is very soft. Add the sugar to the butter and mix. Add the eggs to the butter and mix together.

Gradually incorporate the flour, flicking it onto the mixture, then chop through it until you have a rough dough. Bring together and knead a few times until smooth. Roll into a ball, cover in plastic wrap and refrigerate for 1 hour.

To make the frangipane, beat the butter until soft. Add the icing sugar, almonds and flour and beat well. Add the egg gradually, beating well. Put in a clean bowl, cover with plastic wrap and refrigerate for up to 24 hours.

Preheat the oven to 180°C (350°F/ Gas 4). Roll out the pastry to 2 mm thick and use to line ten 8 cm-wide tartlet tins. Put the frangipane in a piping bag and pipe into the tartlet tins. Put the tins on a baking tray and bake for 10 minutes, or until golden. Cool slightly on a wire rack, then arrange the berries on top. Melt the jam with 1 teaspoon water, sieve out any lumps and brush over the berries.

Makes 10

Mango and passionfruit pies

750 g ready-made or home-made
    sweet shortcrust pastry (see
    page 391)
3 ripe mangoes (900 g), peeled and
    sliced or chopped, or 400 g tin
    mango slices, drained
60 g (¼ cup) passionfruit pulp,
    strained
1 tablespoon custard powder
90 g (⅓ cup) caster sugar
1 egg, lightly beaten
icing sugar, to dust

Preheat the oven to 190°C (375°F/
Gas 5). Grease six 10 cm (top) 8 cm
(base) 3 cm (deep) fluted flan tins or
round pie dishes. Roll out two-thirds
of the pastry between two sheets of
baking paper to a thickness of 3 mm.
Cut out six 13 cm circles. Line the tins
with the circles and trim the edges.
Refrigerate while you make the filling.

Combine the mango, passionfruit,
custard powder and sugar in a bowl.

Roll out the remaining pastry between
two sheets of baking paper to 3 mm
thick. Cut out six 11 cm circles.
Re-roll the pastry trimmings and cut
into shapes for decoration.

Fill the pastry cases with the mango
mixture and brush the edges with
egg. Top with the pastry circles and
press the edges to seal. Trim the
edges and decorate with the pastry
shapes. Brush the tops with beaten
egg and dust with icing sugar.

Bake for 20–25 minutes, or until the
pastry is golden brown. Delicious
served with cream.

Makes 6

Banana cream pie

375 g ready-made or home-made
   shortcrust pastry (see page 390)
80 g (½ cup) dark chocolate bits
   (chocolate chips)
4 egg yolks
125 g (½ cup) caster sugar
½ teaspoon vanilla essence
2 tablespoons custard powder
500 ml (2 cups) milk
40 g unsalted butter, softened
1 teaspoon brandy or rum
3 large ripe bananas, cut into
   3–4 mm slices
sliced banana, extra, to decorate
50 g dark chocolate, grated or
   shaved, to decorate

Roll out the pastry between two sheets of baking paper to line the base of a 23 cm (top) 18 cm (base) 3 cm (deep) pie tin. Remove the top sheet of paper and invert the pastry into the tin (see page 392). Trim the excess. Refrigerate for 20 minutes.

Preheat the oven to 190°C (375°F/ Gas 5). Line the pastry with crumpled baking paper and cover with baking beads or rice. Bake for 10 minutes, remove the paper and beads, then bake for 10 minutes, or until the pastry is dry and cooked through. While still hot, cover with chocolate bits. Leave for 5 minutes, then spread the melted chocolate over the base.

Put the egg yolks, sugar, vanilla and custard powder in a bowl and beat with electric beaters for 2–3 minutes, or until thick. Bring the milk to the boil in a pan over medium heat, remove from the heat and gradually pour into the egg mixture, stirring well. Return the custard filling to the saucepan and bring to the boil, stirring well. Cook for 2 minutes, or until thick. Remove from the heat, stir in the butter and brandy and leave to cool. Arrange the banana slices over the chocolate, then pour over the custard. Decorate with extra banana and the grated chocolate.

Serves 6–8

Nutty fig pie

375 g ready-made or home-made
   shortcrust pastry (see page 390)
200 g (1½ cups) hazelnuts
100 g (⅔ cup) pine nuts
100 g (1 cup) flaked almonds
100 g (⅔ cup) blanched almonds
170 ml (⅔ cup) cream
60 g unsalted butter
90 g (¼ cup) honey
95 g (½ cup) soft brown sugar
150 g dessert figs, cut into quarters
chocolate ice cream, to serve

Preheat the oven to 200°C (400°F/
Gas 6) and grease a 23 cm (top)
18 cm (base) 3 cm (deep) pie tin. Roll
the pastry out between two sheets of
baking paper until large enough to
cover the base and side of the pie tin.
Remove the top sheet and invert the
pastry into the tin, allowing any
excess to hang over. Trim with a knife
and prick the base several times with
a fork. Score the edge with a fork.
Refrigerate for 20 minutes, then bake
for 15 minutes, or until crisp, dry and
lightly golden. Allow to cool.

Bake the hazelnuts on a baking tray
for 8 minutes, or until the skins start
to peel away. Tip into a tea towel and
rub to remove the skins. Place the
pine nuts, flaked almonds and
blanched almonds on a baking tray
and bake for 5–6 minutes, or until
lightly golden.

Place the cream, butter, honey and
brown sugar in a saucepan and stir
over medium heat until the sugar
dissolves and the butter melts.
Remove from the heat and stir in the
nuts and figs. Spoon the mixture
into the pastry case and bake for
30 minutes. Remove and cool until
firm before slicing. Delicious served
with chocolate ice cream.

Serves 8

Apricot and almond tart

375 g ready-made or home-made
   sweet shortcrust pastry (see
   page 391)
200 g (1¼ cups) dried apricots
100 ml brandy or grappa
icing sugar, to dust
crème fraîche or cream, to serve

Almond filling
180 g unsalted butter, softened
180 g (¾ cup) caster sugar
180 g (2 cups) flaked blanched
   almonds
2 eggs
1 teaspoon vanilla extract
1 heaped teaspoon plain flour

Grease a 25 cm loose-bottomed
metal tart tin. Dust the work surface
with flour and roll out the pastry to fit
the tin. Line the tin and trim the edges.
Refrigerate for 15 minutes. Preheat
the oven to 200°C (400°F/Gas 6).

Line the pastry shell with crumpled
baking paper and baking beads and
bake for 12 minutes, then remove the
paper and beads — if the pastry still
looks wet, dry it out in the oven for
5 minutes. Cool for a few minutes.
Reduce the oven to 180°C (350°F/
Gas 4).

Put the dried apricots and brandy in a
saucepan and cook over low heat for
about 5 minutes, or until most of the
liquid has evaporated. Leave to cool.

To make the almond filling, use a food
processor to cream the butter and
sugar until light and pale. Add the
almonds, eggs, vanilla and flour and
briefly blend. If you overbeat it, the
mixture may separate. Spoon the
filling into the pastry shell, then place
the apricots in the shell, arranging
them in two circles, one inside the
other. Bake for 30–40 minutes, or until
the filling is set. Cool and sprinkle with
icing sugar just before serving. Serve
with crème fraîche or cream.

Serves 8

Blackberry pie

500 g ready-made or home-made
   sweet shortcrust pastry (see page
   391)
500 g (4 cups) blackberries
160 g (²/₃ cup) caster sugar
2 tablespoons cornflour
milk, to brush
1 egg, lightly beaten
caster sugar, extra, to sprinkle

Preheat the oven to 200°C (400°F/
Gas 6). Grease a 26 cm (top)
20.5 cm (base) 4.5 cm (deep) ceramic
pie dish. Roll out two-thirds of the
pastry between two sheets of baking
paper until large enough to line the
base and side of the pie dish.
Remove the top paper, invert the
pastry into the dish and press firmly
into place, leaving the excess
overhanging the edges.

Toss the blackberries (if frozen, thaw
and drain well), sugar and cornflour
together in a bowl until well mixed,
then transfer to the pie dish. Roll out
the remaining pastry between two
sheets of baking paper until large
enough to cover the pie. Moisten the
rim of the pie base with milk and
press the pastry lid firmly into place.
Trim and crimp the edges. Brush with
egg and sprinkle with the extra sugar.
Pierce the top of the pie with a knife.

Bake on the bottom shelf of the oven
for 10 minutes. Reduce the oven to
180°C (350°F/Gas 4) and move the
pie to the centre shelf. Bake for
another 30 minutes, or until golden on
top. Cool before serving with cream
or ice cream.

Serves 6

Portuguese custard tarts

155 g (1 1/4 cups) plain flour
25 g copha (white vegetable
  shortening), chopped and softened
30 g unsalted butter, chopped and
  softened
250 g (1 cup) sugar
500 ml (2 cups) milk
3 tablespoons cornflour
1 tablespoon custard powder
4 egg yolks
1 teaspoon vanilla essence

Sift the flour into a bowl. Add 185 ml (3/4 cup) water, or enough to form a soft dough. Gather into a ball, then roll out on baking paper to form a 24 x 30 cm rectangle. Spread the copha over the surface. Roll up from the short edge to form a log.

Roll the dough out into a rectangle again, and spread with the butter. Roll into a log and slice into 12 pieces. Working from the centre outwards, use your fingertips to press each round out to a circle large enough to cover the base and sides of twelve 80 ml (1/3 cup) muffin holes. Press into the tin and refrigerate.

Put the sugar and 80 ml (1/3 cup) water into a pan, and stir over low heat until the sugar dissolves. Mix a little milk with the cornflour and custard powder to form a smooth paste, and add to the pan with the remaining milk, egg yolks and vanilla. Stir over low heat until thickened. Put in a bowl, cover and cool.

Preheat the oven to 220°C (425°F/ Gas 7). Divide the filling among the pastry bases. Bake for 30 minutes, or until the custard is set and the tops have browned. Cool in the tins, then transfer to a wire rack.

Makes 12

Pear and almond flan

155 g (1 ¼ cups) plain flour
90 g unsalted butter, chilled and
chopped
60 g (¼ cup) caster sugar
2 egg yolks

Filling
165 g unsalted butter, softened
160 g (⅔ cup) caster sugar
3 eggs
230 g (2¼ cups) ground almonds
1½ tablespoons plain flour
2 ripe pears, peeled, halved
lengthways with cores removed

Grease a shallow 24 cm round flan tin with a removable base. Put the flour, butter and caster sugar in a food processor and process until the mixture resembles breadcrumbs. Add the egg yolks and about 1 tablespoon of water until the mixture just comes together. Turn out onto a floured surface and gather into a ball. Cover in plastic wrap and refrigerate for 30 minutes. Preheat the oven to 180°C (350°F/Gas 4).

Roll the pastry between baking paper dusted with flour and line the tin with the pastry. Trim off any excess. Prick the base a few times. Blind bake the pastry for 10 minutes (see page 392). Remove the paper and beads and bake for 10 minutes.

To make the filling, mix the butter and sugar with electric beaters for 30 seconds only. Add the eggs one at a time, beating after each addition. Fold in the ground almonds and flour and spread the filling over the cooled base. Cut the pears crossways into 3 mm slices, separate them slightly, then place on top of the tart to form a cross. Bake for 50 minutes, or until the filling has set (the middle may still be a little soft). Cool in the tin, then refrigerate for 2 hours before serving.

Serves 8

Lemon meringue pie

375 g ready-made or home-made
  sweet shortcrust pastry (see page
  391)
30 g (¼ cup) plain flour
30 g (¼ cup) cornflour
250 g (1 cup) caster sugar
185 ml (¾ cup) lemon juice
1 tablespoon grated lemon zest
50 g unsalted butter, chopped
6 egg yolks
1 quantity meringue (see page 393)

Grease a 25 cm (top) 18 cm (base) 3 cm (deep) pie plate. Roll the pastry out between two sheets of baking paper into a 30 cm circle. Invert the pastry into the plate. Trim the edges. Re-roll the pastry trimmings and cut into three 10 x 2 cm strips. Brush the pie rim with water, place the pastry strips around the top and use your fingers to make a decorative edge. Prick over the base with a fork. Cover and refrigerate for 20 minutes. Preheat the oven to 180°C (350°F/Gas 4).

Blind bake the pastry for 15 minutes (see page 392). Remove the beads and bake for 15–20 minutes. Cool.

Increase the oven to 200°C (400°F/ Gas 6). Put the flours, sugar, lemon juice and zest in a pan. Gradually add 315 ml (1¼ cups) water and whisk over medium heat until smooth. Cook, stirring, for 2 minutes, or until thick. Remove from the heat and vigorously whisk in the butter and egg yolks. Return to low heat and stir constantly, for 2 minutes, or until very thick.

Spread the lemon filling into the pastry base, then cover with the meringue, piling high in the centre and making peaks with a knife. Bake for 8–10 minutes, or until lightly browned.

Serves 4–6

Old-fashioned apple pie

Pastry
250 g (2 cups) self-raising flour
85 g (²/₃ cup) cornflour
180 g unsalted butter, chilled and
  cubed
90 g (¹/₃ cup) caster sugar
1 egg, lightly beaten

40 g unsalted butter
6 green apples, peeled, cored and
  thinly sliced
1 tablespoon lemon juice
140 g (³/₄ cup) soft brown sugar
1 teaspoon ground nutmeg
2 tablespoons plain flour mixed with
  60 ml (¹/₄ cup) water
25 g (¹/₄ cup) ground almonds
milk, to brush
sugar, to sprinkle

Lightly grease a 1 litre, 20 cm metal pie dish. Sift the flours into a large bowl and rub in the butter with your fingers until the mixture resembles fine breadcrumbs. Stir in the sugar and a pinch of salt. Make a well, add the egg and mix with a knife, using a cutting action, until the mixture comes together in beads. Put the dough on a floured surface and press into a smooth disc, cover with plastic wrap and refrigerate for 20 minutes.

Use two-thirds of the dough to line the base and side of the dish (see page 392). Roll out the remaining dough to make a lid. Cover and refrigerate for 20 minutes. Preheat the oven to 200°C (400°F/Gas 6) and heat a baking tray.

Melt the butter in a large frying pan, add the apple and toss. Stir in the lemon juice, sugar and nutmeg and cook for 10 minutes, or until tender. Add the flour and water mixture, then the almonds. Bring to the boil and cook, stirring, for 2–3 minutes. Pour into a bowl and cool. Put the apple in the pastry case. Cover with the pastry lid and press lightly onto the rim. Trim the edges and pinch together to seal. Prick over the top, brush with milk and sprinkle with sugar. Bake on the hot tray for 40 minutes, or until golden.

Serves 8

Almond pies

50 g (½ cup) flaked almonds
125 g unsalted butter, softened
125 g (1 cup) icing sugar
125 g (1¼ cups) ground almonds
30 g (¼ cup) plain flour
2 eggs
1 tablespoon rum or brandy
1 teaspoon almond essence
½ teaspoon vanilla essence
4 sheets frozen ready-made puff
  pastry, thawed
1 egg, lightly beaten
sugar, to sprinkle
icing sugar, to dust

Preheat the oven to 200°C (400°F/ Gas 6). Bake the flaked almonds on a baking tray for 2–3 minutes, or until just golden. Remove and return the tray to the oven to keep it hot.

Beat together the butter, icing sugar, ground almonds, flour, eggs, rum, almond essence and vanilla with electric beaters for 2–3 minutes, or until smooth and combined. Fold in the flaked almonds.

Cut out eight 10 cm rounds and eight 11 cm rounds from the puff pastry. Spread the smaller rounds with equal amounts of filling, leaving a 1 cm border. Brush the borders with beaten egg and cover with the tops. Seal the edges with a fork and, if you wish, decorate the tops with shapes cut from pastry scraps.

Pierce with a fork to allow steam to escape. Brush with egg and sprinkle with sugar. Bake on the hot tray for 15–20 minutes, or until the pastry is puffed and golden. Dust with icing sugar before serving.

Makes 8

Peach pie

500 g ready-made or home-made
  sweet shortcrust pastry (see page
  391)
2 x 825 g tins peach slices,
  well-drained
125 g (½ cup) caster sugar
30 g (¼ cup) cornflour
¼ teaspoon almond essence
20 g unsalted butter, chopped
1 tablespoon milk
1 egg, lightly beaten
caster sugar, to sprinkle

Roll out two-thirds of the dough
between two sheets of baking paper
until large enough to line a 23 cm
(top) 18 cm (base) 3 cm (deep) pie tin.
Remove the top sheet of paper and
invert the pastry into the tin. Use a
small ball of pastry to press the pastry
into the tin. Trim any excess pastry
with a knife. Refrigerate for 20 minutes.

Preheat the oven to 200°C (400°F/
Gas 6). Line the pastry with crumpled
baking paper and pour in baking
beads or rice. Bake for 10 minutes,
remove the paper and beads and
return to the oven for 5 minutes, or
until the pastry base is dry and lightly
coloured. Allow to cool.

Mix the peaches, sugar, cornflour and
almond essence in a bowl, then spoon
into the pastry shell. Dot with butter
and moisten the edges with milk.

Roll out the remaining dough to a
25 cm square. Using a fluted pastry
cutter, cut into ten strips 2.5 cm wide.
Lay the strips in a lattice pattern over
the filling, pressing firmly on the edges
and trim. Brush with egg and sprinkle
with sugar. Bake for 10 minutes,
reduce the heat to 180°C (350°F/Gas
4) and bake for 30 minutes, or until
golden. Cool before serving.

Serves 6

Berry ricotta cream tartlets

Pastry
185 g (1½ cups) plain flour
95 g (1 cup) ground almonds
40 g (⅓ cup) icing sugar
125 g unsalted butter, chopped
1 egg, lightly beaten

Filling
200 g (¾ cup) ricotta cheese
1 teaspoon vanilla essence
2 eggs
160 g (⅔ cup) caster sugar
125 ml (½ cup) cream
60 g (½ cup) raspberries
80 g (½ cup) blueberries
icing sugar, to dust

Sift the flour into a bowl, then add the almonds and icing sugar. Rub the butter into the flour with your fingertips until it resembles breadcrumbs. Make a well in the centre, add the egg and mix with a flat-bladed knife, using a cutting action, until the mixture comes together in beads. Gather the dough and put onto a lightly floured surface. Press into a ball, cover with plastic wrap and refrigerate for 30 minutes.

Grease six 8 cm (3 cm deep) loose-bottomed tart tins. Divide the pastry into six and roll each piece out between two sheets of baking paper to fit the base and side of the tins. Press the pastry into the tins, trim the edges and prick the bases with a fork. Refrigerate for 30 minutes. Preheat the oven to 180°C (350°F/Gas 4). Line the pastry with crumpled baking paper and spread with baking beads or rice. Bake for 8–10 minutes, then remove the paper and beads.

Process the ricotta, vanilla, eggs, sugar and cream in a food processor until smooth. Divide the berries and filling among the tarts and bake for 25–30 minutes, or until the filling is just set — the top should be soft but not too wobbly. Cool. Dust with icing sugar and serve.

Serves 6

Pear and apple crumble pie

375 g ready-made or home-made
    shortcrust pastry (see page 390)
3 pears, peeled, cored and sliced
4 Granny Smith apples, peeled, cored
    and sliced
60 g (¼ cup) caster sugar
2 teaspoons grated orange zest
90 g (¾ cup) raisins
90 g (¾ cup) plain flour
95 g (½ cup) soft brown sugar
½ teaspoon ground ginger
90 g unsalted butter
thick (double) cream, to serve

Roll the pastry between two sheets of baking paper until large enough to cover the base and side of a 23 cm (top) 18 cm (base) 3 cm (deep) pie dish. Remove the top baking paper and invert the pastry into the dish. Trim the excess. Cover with plastic wrap and refrigerate for 20 minutes.

Put the sliced fruit in a large pan. Add the sugar, zest and 2 tablespoons water and cook over low heat, stirring occasionally for 20 minutes, or until the fruit is tender but still holding its shape. Remove from the heat, add the raisins and a pinch of salt and mix. Cool, then spoon into the pastry case.

Preheat the oven to 200°C (400°F/Gas 6) and preheat a baking tray. To make the topping, combine the flour, brown sugar and ginger in a bowl and rub in the butter with your fingertips until the mixture resembles coarse breadcrumbs. Sprinkle over the fruit.

Place the pie dish on the hot baking tray, bake for 10 minutes, then reduce the oven temperature to 180°C (350°F/Gas 4) and cook the pie for 40 minutes, or until nicely browned. Cover the pie with foil halfway through if the top is browning too quickly. Serve warm with cream.

Serves 6–8

Key lime pie

375 g ready-made or home-made
   sweet shortcrust pastry (see page
   391)
4 egg yolks
395 g tin condensed milk
125 ml (1/2 cup) lime juice
2 teaspoons grated lime zest
lime slices, to garnish
icing sugar, to dust
whipped cream, to serve

Preheat the oven to 180°C (350°F/
Gas 4). Grease a 23 cm loose-
bottomed flan tin. Roll the dough out
between two sheets of baking paper
until it is large enough to fit into the
pie tin. Remove the top sheet of
paper and invert the pastry into the
tin. Use a small ball of pastry to help
press the pastry into the tin, allowing
any excess to hang over the sides.
Use a small sharp knife to trim away
any extra pastry.

Line the pastry shell with a piece of
crumpled baking paper that is large
enough to cover the base and side of
the tin and pour in some baking
beads or rice. Bake for 10 minutes,
remove the paper and beads and
return the pastry to the oven for
another 4–5 minutes, or until the base
is dry. Leave to cool.

Using electric beaters, beat the egg
yolks, condensed milk, lime juice and
zest in a large bowl for 2 minutes, or
until well combined. Pour into the pie
shell and smooth the surface. Bake
for 20–25 minutes, or until set. Allow
the pie to cool, then refrigerate for
2 hours, or until well chilled. Garnish
with lime slices, dust with sifted icing
sugar and serve with whipped cream.

Serves 6–8

Honey and pine nut tart

Pastry
250 g (2 cups) plain flour
1½ tablespoons icing sugar
115 g unsalted butter, chilled and
  chopped
1 egg, lightly beaten

Filling
175 g (½ cup) honey
115 g unsalted butter, softened
125 g (½ cup) caster sugar
3 eggs, lightly beaten
¼ teaspoon vanilla essence
1 tablespoon almond liqueur
1 teaspoon finely grated lemon zest
1 tablespoon lemon juice
235 g (1½ cups) pine nuts, toasted
  (see page 390)
icing sugar, to dust
crème fraîche or mascarpone, to
  serve

Preheat the oven to 190°C (375°F/ Gas 5) and place a baking tray on the middle shelf. Grease a 23 x 3.5 cm deep loose-bottomed tart tin.

Roll out the pastry between two sheets of baking paper to a 3 mm thick circle. Invert the pastry into the tin, pressing it into the side and base of the tin. Trim any excess. Prick all over the base and chill for 15 minutes. Cut out three leaves about 4 cm long from the pastry scraps. Cover and chill. Line the pastry with baking paper and fill with baking beads. Bake on the tray for 10 minutes, then remove.

Reduce the oven to 180°C (350°F/ Gas 4). To make the filling, heat the honey in a saucepan until runny. Beat the butter and sugar in a bowl until smooth and pale. Gradually add the eggs, beating after each addition. Mix in the honey, vanilla, liqueur, lemon zest and juice and a pinch of salt. Stir in the toasted pine nuts, spoon into the pastry and smooth over. Arrange the pastry leaves in the centre.

Bake on the hot tray for 40 minutes, or until set. Cover the top with foil after 25 minutes. Serve warm, dusted with icing sugar. Serve with crème fraîche or mascarpone.

Serves 6

Raisin pie

600 g ready-made or home-made
  sweet shortcrust pastry (see page
  391)
80 ml (⅓ cup) orange juice
2 tablespoons lemon juice
320 g (2½ cups) raisins
140 g (¾ cup) soft brown sugar
½ teaspoon mixed spice
30 g (¼ cup) cornflour
1 teaspoon finely grated lemon zest
1 teaspoon finely grated orange zest
1 egg, lightly beaten
1 tablespoon sugar, to sprinkle

Preheat the oven to 190°C (375°F/
Gas 5) and heat a baking tray. Grease
a 23 cm (top) 18 cm (base) 3 cm
(deep) pie tin. Roll out two-thirds of
the pastry between two sheets of
baking paper to fit the base and side
of the dish. Remove the top paper
and invert the pastry into the tin,
pressing it into the tin. Trim the excess.
Chill the base and remaining pastry.

Combine the citrus juices, raisins and
250 ml (1 cup) water in a pan. Boil
over high heat, stirring occasionally,
for 2 minutes. Remove from the heat.

Mix the brown sugar, mixed spice and
cornflour in a bowl. Add 125 ml
(½ cup) water and mix until smooth.
Slowly stir into the raisin mixture and
return the pan to the stove over high
heat. Boil, stirring, then reduce to
a simmer, stirring occasionally, for
5 minutes, or until it thickens. Stir in
the citrus zest and cool for 30 minutes.

Roll out the remaining pastry to cover
the pie. Fill the base with the raisin
mixture, brush the edges with the egg
and cover with the pastry top. Pinch
the edges together and make a few
small holes. Brush with egg, sprinkle
with sugar and bake for 40 minutes,
or until golden. Serve warm or cold.

Serves 6–8

Lime and blueberry pie

375 g ready-made or home-made
  sweet shortcrust pastry (see page
  391)
3 eggs
125 g (1/2 cup) caster sugar
60 ml (1/4 cup) buttermilk
1 tablespoon lime juice
2 teaspoons grated lime zest
2 tablespoons custard powder
250 g (1²/₃ cups) blueberries
icing sugar, to dust

Roll out the pastry between two sheets of baking paper to line a 23 cm (top) 18 cm (base) 3 cm (deep) pie tin. Remove the top paper and invert the pastry into the tin. Use a small ball of pastry to press the pastry into the tin. Trim any excess pastry. Refrigerate for 20 minutes.

Preheat the oven to 200°C (400°F/ Gas 6). Line the base and side of the pastry with crumpled baking paper and pour in baking beads or rice. Bake for 10 minutes, remove the paper and beads and bake for 4–5 minutes, or until the base is dry and lightly coloured. Cool slightly. Reduce the oven to 180°C (350°F/Gas 4).

To make the filling, beat the eggs and caster sugar in a bowl with electric beaters until the mixture is thick and pale. Add the buttermilk, lime juice, zest and sifted custard powder. Stir until combined, then spoon into the pastry shell. Bake for 15 minutes, then reduce the temperature to 160°C (315°F/Gas 2–3) and cook for another 20–25 minutes, or until the filling has coloured slightly and is set. Cool (the filling will sink while cooling), then top with the blueberries. Dust with sifted icing sugar and serve.

Serves 6–8

Apple galette

1 sheet frozen puff pastry, thawed
80 g (¼ cup) apricot jam
1 Granny Smith apple
2 teaspoons demerara sugar

Preheat the oven to 210°C (415°F/ Gas 6–7). Place a baking tray in the oven to heat. Trim the corners from the pastry to make a neat circle (use a large plate as a guide if you like).

Place the jam in a small saucepan and stir over low heat to warm through and thin. Strain through a sieve to remove any chunks of fruit and brush over the puff pastry, leaving a 1.5 cm border.

Peel, halve and core the apple, and cut into 2 mm thick slices. Arrange over the pastry in an overlapping circular pattern, leaving a 1.5 cm border around the edge. Sprinkle evenly with the sugar.

Carefully place the galette on a lightly greased tray and bake for 35 minutes, or until the edge of the pastry is well browned and puffed.

Serves 6

Pumpkin pie

Pastry
155 g (1 ¼ cups) plain flour
100 g unsalted butter, chilled and
 cubed
2 teaspoons caster sugar
4 tablespoons iced water

750 g butternut pumpkin, cubed,
 boiled and mashed, then pushed
 through a sieve, cooled
2 eggs, lightly beaten
185 g (1 cup) soft brown sugar
80 ml (⅓ cup) cream
1 tablespoon sweet sherry or brandy
½ teaspoon ground ginger
½ teaspoon ground nutmeg
1 teaspoon ground cinnamon

Sift the flour into a bowl and rub in the butter with your fingertips until the mixture resembles breadcrumbs. Mix in the caster sugar. Make a well in the centre, add almost all the water and mix with a flat-bladed knife, using a cutting action, until the mixture comes together in beads — add more water if needed. Gather the dough and put on a lightly floured surface. Press into a ball and flatten slightly. Cover in plastic wrap. Refrigerate for 20 minutes.

Roll out the pastry between two sheets of baking paper large enough to cover the base and side of a 23 cm (top) 18 cm (base) 3 cm (deep) pie dish. Line the dish with pastry, trim the excess and crimp the edges with a fork. Cover with plastic wrap and refrigerate for 20 minutes. Preheat the oven to 180°C (350°F/Gas 4). Line the pastry shell with crumpled baking paper. Pour in baking beads and bake for 10 minutes, then remove the paper and beads. Cook for 10 minutes, or until lightly golden. Cool.

Whisk the eggs and sugar in a bowl. Stir in the cooled pumpkin, cream, sherry and the spices. Pour into the pastry shell and bake for 1 hour, or until set — cover the edges with foil if overbrowning. Cool before serving.

Serves 6–8

Apple tarte tatin

100 g unsalted butter, chopped
185 g (3/4 cup) sugar
6 large pink lady, fuji or golden
  delicious apples, peeled, cored and
  quartered
1 sheet ready-made puff pastry
thick (double) cream or ice cream,
  to serve

Preheat the oven to 220°C (425°F/ Gas 7). Lightly grease a 23 cm shallow cake tin. Melt the unsalted butter in a frying pan, add the sugar and cook, stirring, over medium heat for 4–5 minutes, or until the sugar starts to caramelize and turn brown. Continue to cook, stirring, until the caramel turns golden brown.

Add the apple to the pan and cook over low heat for 20–25 minutes, or until it starts to turn golden brown. Carefully turn the apple over and cook the other side until evenly coloured. Cook off any liquid that comes out of the apple over a higher heat. The caramel should be sticky rather than runny. Remove from the heat. Using tongs, arrange the hot apple in circles in the tin and pour the sauce over it.

Place the pastry over the apple to cover it, tucking the pastry down firmly at the edges using the end of a spoon. Bake for 30–35 minutes, or until the pastry is cooked. Leave the tarte tatin to stand for 15 minutes before inverting onto a serving plate. Remove the paper and serve warm or cold with thick cream or ice cream.

Serves 6

Tarte au citron

Pastry
350 g (2¾ cups) plain flour
small pinch of salt
150 g unsalted butter
100 g (¾ cup) icing sugar
2 eggs, beaten

Filling
4 eggs
2 egg yolks
275 g (1¼ cups) caster sugar
190 ml (¾ cup) thick (double) cream
250 ml (1 cup) lemon juice
finely grated zest of 3 lemons

To make the pastry, sift the flour and salt onto a work surface and make a well. Put the butter into the well and work, using a pecking action with your fingertips and thumb, until it is very soft. Add the sugar to the butter and mix. Add the eggs to the butter and mix. Gradually incorporate the flour, flicking it onto the mixture, then chop through it until you have a rough dough. Bring together, knead a few times to make a smooth dough, then roll into a ball. Cover in plastic wrap and refrigerate for at least 1 hour.

Preheat the oven to 190°C (375°F/ Gas 5). Roll out the pastry to line a 23 cm round loose-based fluted tart tin. Chill for 20 minutes. To make the filling, whisk together the eggs, egg yolks and sugar. Add the cream, whisking all the time, then the lemon juice and zest.

Blind bake the pastry (see page 392) for 10 minutes, remove the paper and bake for 3–5 minutes, or until the pastry is just cooked. Remove from the oven and reduce the oven to 150°C (300°F/Gas 2). Put the tin on a baking tray and carefully pour the filling into the pastry case. Return to the oven for 35–40 minutes, or until set. Cool before serving.

Serves 8

Chocolate fudge pecan pie

Pastry
155 g (1¼ cups) plain flour
2 tablespoons cocoa powder
2 tablespoons soft brown sugar
100 g unsalted butter, chilled and cubed
2–3 tablespoons iced water

200 g (2 cups) pecan nuts, roughly chopped
100 g dark chocolate, chopped
95 g (½ cup) soft brown sugar
170 ml (⅔ cup) light or dark corn syrup
3 eggs, lightly beaten
2 teaspoons vanilla essence

Grease a 23 cm (top) 18 cm (base) 3 cm (deep) pie dish. Sift the flour, cocoa and sugar into a bowl and rub in the butter with your fingertips until the mixture resembles fine breadcrumbs. Make a well, add almost all the water and mix with a knife, adding more water if necessary.

Gather the dough together and lift onto a sheet of baking paper. Press the dough into a disc and refrigerate for 20 minutes. Roll out the pastry between two sheets of baking paper to fit the dish. Line the dish and trim the edges. Refrigerate for 20 minutes.

Preheat the oven to 180°C (350°F/ Gas 4). Cover the pastry with crumpled baking paper and fill with baking beads or rice. Bake for 15 minutes, then remove the paper and beads and bake for 15–20 minutes, or until the base is dry. Cool completely.

Place the pie dish on a flat baking tray to catch any drips. Spread the pecans and chocolate over the pastry base. Combine the sugar, corn syrup, eggs and vanilla in a jug and whisk together with a fork. Pour into the pastry shell, and bake for 45 minutes (the filling will still be a bit wobbly, but will set on cooling). Cool before cutting to serve.

Serves 6

Cherry pie

500 g ready-made or home-made
  sweet shortcrust pastry (see
  page 391)
2 x 425 g tins seedless black
  cherries, drained well
60 g (⅓ cup) soft brown sugar
1½ teaspoons ground cinnamon
1 teaspoon finely grated lemon zest
1 teaspoon finely grated orange zest
1–2 drops almond essence
25 g (¼ cup) ground almonds
1 egg, lightly beaten

Preheat the oven to 190°C (375°F/
Gas 5). Roll out two-thirds of the
dough between two sheets of baking
paper to form a circle large enough to
fit a 22 cm (top) 20 cm (base) 2 cm
(deep) pie plate. Remove the top
sheet of baking paper and invert the
pastry into the pie plate. Cut away the
excess pastry with a small sharp
knife. Roll out the remaining pastry
large enough to cover the pie.
Refrigerate, covered in plastic wrap,
for 20 minutes.

Place the cherries, sugar, cinnamon,
lemon and orange zests, and almond
essence in a bowl and mix to coat
the cherries.

Line the pastry base with the ground
almonds. Spoon in the filling, brush
the pastry edges with beaten egg,
and cover with the pastry lid. Use a
fork to seal the edges pastry. Cut four
slits in the top of the pie to allow
steam to escape, then brush the
pastry with beaten egg. Bake for
1 hour, or until the pastry is golden
and the juices are bubbling through
the slits in the pastry. Serve warm.

Serves 6

Walnut pie with caramel sauce

Pastry
250 g (2 cups) plain flour
180 g unsalted butter, chilled and
  cubed
40 g (1/3 cup) icing sugar
1 egg yolk
3–4 tablespoons iced water

Filling
2 eggs
210 g (1 cup) caster sugar
150 g (1 1/2 cups) walnuts, finely
  chopped

1 egg yolk, lightly beaten
icing sugar, to dust
walnuts, to garnish
1 quantity caramel sauce (see page
  393)

Sift the flour and 1/2 teaspoon salt into a large bowl and rub in the butter until the mixture resembles breadcrumbs. Mix in the icing sugar. Make a well, add the egg yolk and almost all the water and mix with a flat-bladed knife, using a cutting action, until the mixture comes together in beads. Lift out onto a floured surface. Press into a ball and flatten slightly. Cover in plastic wrap. Refrigerate for 20 minutes.

Preheat the oven to 180°C (350°F/ Gas 4). Grease a fluted 36 x 11 cm pie tin. Place the eggs and sugar in a bowl and beat with a spoon or whisk for 2 minutes. Stir in the walnuts.

Divide the dough into two portions, one slightly larger than the other. Line the base and side of the tin with the larger portion (see page 392). Cover in plastic wrap and refrigerate. Roll out the remaining pastry for a lid.

Pour the walnut filling into the shell, brush the rim with egg yolk and cover with the lid, pressing the edges to seal. Trim the edge. Make a steam hole in the top. Brush with egg yolk and bake for 30–35 minutes. Cool at room temperature for at least 1 hour. Dust with icing sugar and sprinkle with walnuts. Drizzle with caramel sauce.

Serves 6–8

Basics

Toasting nuts

Toasting nuts before use enhances their flavour.

Spread the nuts on a baking tray and toast in a 180°C (350°F/Gas 4) oven for 5–8 minutes, or until they are lightly coloured. Once they start to brown, nuts burn very quickly, so watch them carefully.

Melting chocolate

When melting chocolate, always use a clean, dry bowl. Water or moisture will make the chocolate seize (turn into a thick mass that won't melt), and overheating will make it scorch and taste bitter.

To melt chocolate, chop it into small even-sized pieces and place in a heatproof bowl. Bring a saucepan of water to the boil, then remove from the heat. Sit the bowl over the saucepan of water — make sure the bowl doesn't touch the water and that no water or steam gets into the bowl or the chocolate will seize. Leave the chocolate to soften a little, then stir until smooth and melted.

Remove the chocolate from the saucepan to cool, or leave in place over the hot water if you want to keep the chocolate liquid.

Shortcrust pastry

This recipe makes about 375 g of shortcrust pastry, which is enough to line the base of a 23 cm pie dish, or just the top. Simply double the recipe to make 750 g of pastry.

To make 375 g of shortcrust pastry you will need 250 g (2 cups) plain flour, 125 g chilled butter, chopped into small pieces, and 2–3 tablespoons iced water. To line the top and base, you will need 600 g of pastry, and for this you need 400 g plain flour, 180 g chilled butter, chopped into small pieces, and 3–4 tablespoons iced water.

Sift the flour and ¼ teaspoon salt into a large bowl. Sifting the flour aerates the dough and helps make the finished pastry crisp and light.

Add the chopped butter and rub it into the flour using your fingertips (not your palms as they tend to be too warm) until the mixture resembles fine breadcrumbs. As you rub the butter into the flour, lift it up high and let it fall back into the bowl. If applicable, stir in the other dry ingredients such as sugar (if making sweet pastry).

Make a well in the centre, add nearly all the water and mix with a flat-bladed knife, using a cutting rather than a stirring action. The mixture will come together in small beads of dough. If necessary, add more water, a teaspoon at a time, until the dough comes together. Test the dough by pinching a little piece between your fingers — if it doesn't hold together, it needs more water. Use just enough to hold the pastry together — if it is too wet it will toughen and may shrink on baking; if too dry, it will be crumbly.

Gently gather the dough together and lift out onto a lightly floured surface. Press the dough into a ball and then flatten it slightly — don't knead or handle the dough too much.

Cover in plastic wrap and refrigerate for 20–30 minutes — this makes it easier to roll out the dough and helps prevent shrinkage during cooking.

Rich shortcrust pastry
This pastry is often used for fruit pies, flans and tarts as it gives a richer, crisper crust.

To transform a basic shortcrust pastry into a rich one, gradually add a beaten egg yolk to the flour with 2–3 tablespoons iced water. Mix with a flat-bladed knife, as described in the technique for shortcrust pastry on page 390.

Sweet shortcrust pastry
Follow the directions to make the shortcrust pastry and add 2 tablespoons caster or icing sugar after the butter has been rubbed into the flour. If preferred, you can also add egg yolks to enrich the pastry (see rich shortcrust pastry).

Food processor shortcrust
Shortcrust pastry can be made quickly and successfully with a food processor. The obvious advantage is its speed but, also, you don't handle the pastry much so it stays cool.

Process the flour and cold chopped butter in short bursts, using the pulse button if your machine has one, until the mixture resembles fine breadcrumbs. While the processor is running, add a teaspoon of water at a time until the dough holds together. Process in short bursts again and don't overprocess or the pastry will toughen and shrink while cooking. You will know you have overworked the pastry if it forms a ball in the processor — it should just come together in clumps.

Gather it into a ball on a lightly floured surface, flatten it into a disc and wrap in plastic wrap, then refrigerate for 20–30 minutes.

Lining the tin with pastry

Remove the dough from the refrigerator. Roll out the dough between two sheets of baking paper or plastic wrap, or on a lightly floured surface. Roll from the centre outwards, rotating the dough, rather than backwards and forwards

If you used baking paper to roll out the pastry, remove the top sheet and carefully invert the pastry over the tin, centre it and then peel away the paper. If you rolled out the pastry on a floured surface, roll the pastry back over the rolling pin so it is hanging, then ease it into the tin.

Once the pastry is in the tin, quickly lift up the sides so they don't break over the sharp edges of the tin. Use a small ball of excess dough to help ease and press the pastry shell into the side of the tin.

Allow the excess pastry to hang over the side and, if using a flan tin, roll the rolling pin over the top of the tin to cut off the excess pastry. If using a glass or ceramic pie dish, use a small sharp knife to cut away the excess pastry. If the pie or tart is to have a pastry lid, leave the excess pastry hanging over the edges of the dish — this can be trimmed once the pastry lid is in place.

However gently you handle the dough, it is bound to shrink a little, so let it sit slightly above the side of the tin. If you rolled off the excess pastry with a rolling pin, you may find the pastry has bunched down the sides a little — press the pastry with your thumbs to flatten and lift it.

Refrigerate in the tin for 15 minutes to relax the pastry and prevent or minimize shrinkage.

Blind baking

If the pastry is to have a moist filling, it will probably require partial blind baking to prevent the base from becoming soggy.

When blind baking, the pastry needs some weights put on it to prevent it rising. Cover the base and side of the pastry shell with a piece of crumpled baking or greaseproof paper. Pour in some baking beads, dried beans or uncooked rice.

Bake the pastry shell for the recommended time (usually about 10 minutes), then remove the paper and beads and return the pastry to the oven for 10–15 minutes, or as specified in the recipe, until the base is dry with no greasy patches. Allow to cool completely.

Cooked filling should also be cooled before putting it in the pastry shell to prevent soggy pastry.

Making and testing sugar syrup

When making sugar syrup, put the sugar and water (or other liquid ingredients) into a saucepan and stir over low heat until the sugar dissolves. It is important that the sugar has dissolved completely before raising the heat. Bring to a rolling boil, boiling for the time specified in the recipe. Do not stir the liquid once it is boiling. Use a wet pastry brush to brush the side of the pan to prevent crystals forming.

For the home cook, a sugar thermometer is helpful in determining the exact temperature and stages of the boiled sugar syrup. The correct temperature is very important, or the mixture will not set properly. If you don't have a thermometer, the syrup can be tested by dropping about 1/4 teaspoon of the syrup into a glass or bowl of iced water, then moulding the ball between your fingers.

At soft ball (112–116°C/234–240°F) stage, a blob of syrup when dropped in cold water will form a very soft ball, but will lose its shape in the air.

At firm ball (118–121°C/245–250°F), the syrup will be firmer but still pliable and will lose its shape in the air.

At hard ball (121–130°C/250–265°F) stage, a blob of syrup will form a very firm but pliable ball that will hold its shape at room temperature.

At soft crack (130–143°C/265–290°F) stage, the ball of sugar will stretch to form slightly sticky threads.

At hard crack (143–157°C/290–315°F), the ball can be stretched to form brittle threads.

Meringue

To make one quantity of meringue, beat 6 egg whites and a pinch of cream of tartar in a clean, dry bowl with electric beaters until soft peaks form. Gradually pour in 340 g (1 1/2 cups) caster sugar, beating until the meringue is thick and glossy.

Caramel sauce

To make one quantity of caramel sauce, put 40 g unsalted butter, 230 g (1 1/4 cups) soft brown sugar, 2 teaspoons vanilla essence, 200 ml (3/4 cup) cream in a saucepan and cook, stirring, for 5 minutes, or until the sauce has thickened.

Index

Index

Index

Index

Photographers: Alan Benson, Cris Cordeiro, Craig Cranko, Joe Filshie, Jared Fowler, Ian Hofstetter, Chris L. Jones, Tony Lyons, Andre Martin, Luis Martin, Valerie Martin, Rob Reichenfeld, Brett Stevens

Food Stylists: Marie-Hélène Clauzon, Jane Collins, Carolyn Fienberg, Mary Harris, Sarah de Nardi, Georgina Dolling, Katy Holder, Cherise Koch, Michelle Noerianto, Sarah O'Brien, Sally Parker

Food Preparation: Rekha Arnott, Michelle Earl, Justin Finlay, Jo Glynn, Sonia Grieg, Justine Johnson, Michelle Lawton, Valli Little, Ben Masters, Kerrie Mullins, Kate Murdoch, Briget Palmer, Justine Poole, Julie Ray, Christine Sheppard, Angela Tregonning

Published by Murdoch Books® a division of Murdoch Magazines Pty Ltd,
GPO Box 1203, Sydney NSW 2001

Editorial Director: Diana Hill
Editors: Katharine Gasparini, Kim Rowney, Gordana Trifunovic
Creative Director: Marylouise Brammer Designer: Michelle Cutler
Photographer (chapter openers): Jared Fowler Stylist (chapter openers): Cherise Koch
Production: Fiona Byrne Picture Librarian: Anne Ferrier, Tom Pender

Chief Executive: Juliet Rogers
Publisher: Kay Scarlett

National Library of Australia Cataloguing-in-Publication Data:
Sweet Food. Includes Index.
ISBN 1 74045 204 6
1. Desserts. 2. Cookery
641.86

Printed by Tien Wah Press
PRINTED IN SINGAPORE

You may find cooking times vary depending on the oven you are using. For fan-forced ovens,
as a general rule, set the oven temperature to 20°C lower than indicated in the recipe.
We have used 20 ml tablespoon measures. If you are using a 15 ml tablespoon, for most recipes the
difference will not be noticeable. However, for recipes using small amounts of flour and cornflour, add an
extra teaspoon for each tablespoon specified. We have used 60 g (Grade 3) eggs in all recipes.

IMPORTANT: Those who might be at risk from the effects of salmonella poisoning (the elderly, pregnant
women, young children and those suffering from immune deficiency diseases) should consult their GP
with any concerns about eating raw eggs.

Published by:	UK
AUSTRALIA	Murdoch Books UK Ltd
Murdoch Books® Australia	Ferry House
GPO Box 1203	51–57 Lacy Road
Sydney NSW 2001	London SW15 1PR
Phone: (612) 4352 7000	Phone: (020) 8355 1480
Fax: (612) 4352 7026	Fax: (020) 8355 1499